THE BATTLE
OF THE SOMME
JOHN BUCHAN

AUTHOR OF "GREENMANTLE"
"NELSON'S HISTORY OF THE WAR," etc., etc.

THE
BATTLE OF THE SOMME
JOHN BUCHAN

ENTRANCE TO A CAPTURED
GERMAN DUG-OUT

THE
BATTLE *of the* SOMME

BY

JOHN BUCHAN

AUTHOR OF "GREENMANTLE," "THE THIRTY-NINE STEPS,"
"THE POWER HOUSE," ETC.

WITH MAPS AND ILLUSTRATIONS

NEW YORK
GEORGE H. DORAN COMPANY

c/1917
i, √

COPYRIGHT, 1917,
BY GEORGE H. DORAN COMPANY

PRINTED IN THE UNITED STATES OF AMERICA

CONTENTS

•

ILLUSTRATIONS

MAPS

THE BATTLE OF THE SOMME

THE BATTLE
OF THE SOMME

CHAPTER I

PRELIMINARIES

The Picardy Landscape—The *Santerre*—The Somme Front before
Midsummer 1916—The German Situation—Why a Shorten-
ing of the Line was Impossible—The German Position on the
Somme—The Allied Plan—German Dispositions—The New British Army—Its Quality—Its Munitionment—British Dispositions—
French Dispositions—The Great Bombardment—Trench Raids
and Gas Attacks—The Morning of the Attack, 1st July.

FROM Arras southward the Western battle-
front left the coalpits and sour fields of the
Artois and entered the pleasant region of
Picardy. The great crook of the Upper Somme
and the tributary vale of the Ancre intersect a rolling tableland, dotted with little towns and furrowed
by a hundred shallow chalk streams. Nowhere does
the land rise higher than 500 feet, but a trivial
swell—such is the nature of the landscape—may
carry the eye for thirty miles. There are few detached farms, for it is a country of peasant culti-
vators who cluster in villages. Not a hedge breaks
the long roll of cornlands, and till the higher ground
is reached the lines of tall poplars flanking the great

13

Roman highroads are the chief landmarks. At the lift of country between Somme and Ancre copses patch the slopes, and sometimes a church spire is seen above the trees from some woodland hamlet. The Somme winds in a broad valley between chalk bluffs, faithfully dogged by a canal—a curious river which strains, like the Oxus, "through matted rushy isles," and is sometimes a lake and sometimes an expanse of swamp. The Ancre is such a stream as may be found in Wiltshire, with good trout in its pools. On a hot midsummer day the slopes are ablaze with yellow mustard, red poppies, and blue cornflowers; and to one coming from the lush flats of Flanders, or the "black country" of the Pas de Calais, or the dreary levels of Champagne, or the strange melancholy Verdun hills, this land wears a habitable and cheerful air, as if remote from the oppression of war.

The district is known as the Santerre. Some derive the name from *sana terra*—the healthy land; others from *sarta terra*—the cleared land. Some say it is *sancta terra,* for Peter the Hermit was a Picard, and the piety of the Crusaders enriched the place with a thousand relics and a hundred noble churches. But there are those—and they have much to say for themselves—who read the name *sang terre* —the bloody land, for the Picard was the Gascon of the north, and the countryside is an old cockpit of war. It was the seat of the government of Clovis and Charlemagne. It was ravaged by the Normans, and time and again by the English. There Louis XI. and Charles the Bold fought their battles; it suffered terribly in the Hundred Years' War; German and Spaniard, the pandours of Eugene and the

SIR DOUGLAS HAIG AND
LIEUTENANT-GENERAL SIR PERTAB SINGH

INFANTRY GOING INTO ACTION

ROAD MAKING ON THE BATTLEFIELD

Cossacks of Alexander marched across its fields; from the walls of Peronne the last shot was fired in the campaign of 1814. And in the greatest war of all it was destined to be the theatre of a struggle compared with which its ancient conflicts were like the brawls of a village fair.

Till Midsummer in 1916 the Picardy front had shown little activity. Since that feverish September when de Castelnau had extended on the Allies' left, and Maud'huy beyond de Castelnau, in the great race for the North Sea, there had been no serious action. Just before the Battle of Verdun began the Germans made a feint south of the Somme and gained some ground at Frise and Dompierre. There had been local raids and local bombardments, but the trenches on both sides were good, and a partial advance offered few attractions to either. Amiens was miles behind one front, vital points like St. Quentin and Cambrai and La Fère were far behind the other. In that region only a very great and continuous offensive would offer any strategic results. In July 1915 the British took over most of the line from Arras to the Somme, and on the whole they had a quiet winter in their new trenches. This long stagnation led to one result: it enabled the industrious Germans to excavate the chalk hills on which they lay into a fortress which they believed to be impregnable. Their position was naturally strong, and they strengthened it by every device which science could provide. Their High Command might look uneasily at the Aubers ridge and Lens and Vimy, but it had no doubts about the Albert heights.

The German plan in the West after the first offensive had been checked at the Marne and Ypres, was to hold their front with abundant guns but the bare minimum of men, and use their surplus forces to win a decision in the East. This scheme was foiled by the heroic steadfastness of Russia's retreat, which surrendered territory freely but kept her armies in being. During the winter of 1915-16 the German High Command were growing anxious. They saw that their march to the Dvina and their adventure in the Balkans had failed to shake the resolution of their opponents. They were aware that the Allies had learned with some exactness the lesson of eighteen months of war, and that even now they were superior in men, and would presently be on an equality in munitions. Moreover, the Allied Command was becoming concentrated and shaking itself free from its old passion for divergent operations. Our generals had learned the wisdom of the order of the King of Syria to his captains: "Fight neither with small nor great but only with the King of Israel"; and the King of Israel did not welcome the prospect.

Now, to quote a famous saying of General Foch, "A weakening force must always be attacking," and from the beginning of 1916 the Central Powers were forced into a continuous offensive. Their economic strength was draining steadily. Their people had been told that victory was already won, and were asking what had become of the fruits of it. They feared greatly the coming Allied offensive, for they knew that it would be simultaneous on all fronts, and they cast about for a means of frustrating it. That was the main reason of the great Verdun

assault. Germany hoped, with the obtuseness that
has always marked her estimate of other races, so
to weaken the field strength of France that no future
blow would be possible, and the French nation,
weary and dispirited, would incline to peace. She
hoped, in any event, to lure the Allies into a premature counter-attack, so that their great offensive
might go off at half-cock and be defeated piece-
meal.

None of these things happened. Pétain at
Verdun handled the defence like a master. With
a wise parsimony he refused to use up any
unit. When a division had suffered it was taken out
of the line and replaced by a fresh one, so that none
of the *cadres* were destroyed. He was willing enough
to yield ground, if only the enemy paid his price.
His aim was not to hold territory, but to cripple the
German field army, and his plan succeeded. The
German force was, as the French say, *accroché* at
Verdun, and was compelled to go on long after any
hope of true success had vanished. The place became a trap where Germany was bleeding to death.
Meanwhile, with the full assent of General Joffre,
the Generalissimo in the West, the British armies
made no movement. They were biding their time.

Early in June the Austrian attack on the Tren-
tino had been checked by Italy, and suddenly—in
the East—Russia swung forward to a surprising
victory. Within a month nearly half a million
Austrians had been put out of action, and the dis-
tressed armies of the Dual Monarchy called on
Germany for help. The inevitable von Hindenburg
was brought into play, and such divisions as could
be spared were dispatched from the West. At this

moment, when the grip was tightening in the East, France and Britain made ready for a supreme effort.

Germany's situation was intricate and uneasy. She had no large surplus of men immediately available at her interior depots. The wounded who were ready again for the line and the young recruits from the 1917 class were all needed to fill up the normal wastage in her ranks. She might create new divisions, but it would be mainly done by skimming the old. She had no longer any great mass of free strategic reserves. Most had been sucked into the maelstrom of Verdun or dispatched east to von Hindenburg. At the best, she had a certain number of divisions which represented a local and temporary surplus in some particular area. Beyond these she could only get reinforcements by the process known as "milking the line"—taking out a battalion here and a battalion there—an expedient both cumbrous and wasteful, for these battalions were not fresh troops, and their removal was bound to leave many parts of her front perilously thin. Germany in the West was holding a huge salient—from the North Sea to Soissons, and from Soissons to Verdun. If a wedge were driven in on one side the whole apex would be in danger. The Russian field army could retire safely from Warsaw and Vilna, because it was mobile and lightly equipped, but an army which had been stationary for eighteen months and had relied mainly upon its fortifications would be apt to find a Sedan in any rapid and extensive retirement. The very strength of the German front in the West constituted its weakness. A breach in a fluid line may be mended, but a breach in a rigid and most intricate front is difficult to fill unless there are large

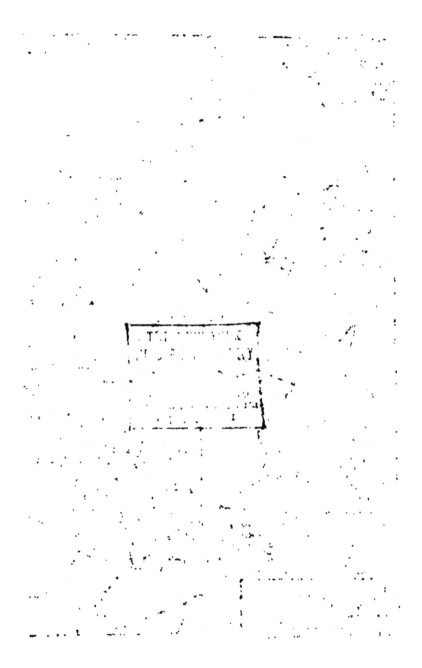

numbers of men available for the task or unlimited time. We have seen that there were no such large numbers, and it was likely that the Allies would see that there was no superfluity of leisure.

The path of wisdom for Germany in June, it might be argued with some force, was to fall back in good order to a much shortened line, which with her numbers might be strongly held. There is reason to believe that soon after the beginning of the Allied bombardment some such policy was considered. The infantry commanders of the 17th Corps were warned to be prepared for long marches and heavy rearguard fighting, instructions were given for holding bridgeheads well in the rear, and officers were advised that the retreat might be either a retirement at ease or a withdrawal under pressure from the enemy. Had such a course been taken it would have been unfortunate for the Allied plans. But such a course was not easy. The foolish glorification after the naval battle of 31st May forbade it. The German people had been buoyed up under the discomfort of the British blockade by tales of decisive successes in the field. The German Chancellor had appealed to his enemies to look at the map, to consider the extent of German territorial gains, and to admit that they were beaten. He was one of those who did not fulfil Foch's definition of military wisdom. "The true soldier is the man who ignores that science of geographical points which is alien to war, which is the negation of war and the sure proof of decadence, the man who knows and follows one vital purpose—to smash the enemy's field force."

Yet, in spite of this weakness in the strategic

situation, the German stronghold in the West was still formidable in the extreme. From Arras southward they held in the main the higher ground. The front consisted of a strong first position, with firing, support, and reserve trenches, and a labyrinth of deep dug-outs; a less strong intermediate line covering the field batteries; and a second position some distance behind, which was of much the same strength as the first. Behind lay fortified woods and villages which could be readily linked up with trench lines to form third and fourth positions. The attached trench map will give some idea of the amazing complexity of the German defences. They were well served by the great network of railways which radiate from La Fère and Laon, Cambrai, and St. Quentin, and many new light lines had been constructed. They had ample artillery and shells, endless machine guns, and consummate skill in using them. It was a fortress to which no front except the West could show a parallel. In the East the line was patchy and not continuous. The Russian soldiers who in the early summer were brought to France stared with amazement at a ramification of trenches compared with which the lines in Poland and Galicia were like hurried improvisations.

The German purpose in the event of an attack was purely defensive. It was to hold their ground, to maintain the mighty forts on which they had spent so many months of labour, to beat off the assault at whatever cost. In that section of their front, at any rate, they were resolved to be a stone wall and not a spear point.

The aim of the Allied Command must be clearly understood. It was not to recover so many square

miles of France; it was not to take Bapaume or
Peronne or St. Quentin; it was not even in the
strict sense to carry this or that position. All these
things were subsidiary and would follow in due
course, provided the main purpose succeeded. That
purpose was simply to exercise a steady and continued pressure on a certain section of the enemy's
front.

For nearly two years the world had been full
of theories as to the possibility of breaking the German line. Many months before critics had pointed
out the futility of piercing that line on too narrow
a front, since all that was produced thereby was
an awkward salient. It was clear that any
breach must be made on a wide front, which would
allow the attacking wedge to manœuvre in the gap,
and prevent reinforcements from coming up quickly
enough to reconstitute the line behind. But this
view took too little account of the strength of the
German fortifications. No doubt a breach could
be made; but its making would be desperately
costly, for no bombardment could destroy all the
defensive lines, and infantry in the attack would
be somewhere or other faced with unbroken wire
and unshaken parapets. Gradually it had been
accepted that an attack should proceed by stages,
with, as a prelude to each, a complete artillery
preparation, and that, since the struggle must be
long drawn out, fresh troops should be used at each
stage.

These were the tactics of the Germans at Verdun, and they were obviously right. Why, then,
did the attack on Verdun fail? In the first place,
because after the first week the assault became

spasmodic and the great plan fell to pieces. Infantry were used wastefully in hopeless rushes. The pressure was relaxed for days on end, and the defence was allowed to reorganise itself. The second reason, of which the first was a consequence, was that Germany, after the initial onslaught, had not the necessary superiority either in numbers or *moral* or guns. At the Somme the Allies did not intend to relax their pressure, and their strength was such that they believed that, save in the event of abnormal weather conditions, they could keep it continuously at a high potential.

A strategical problem is not, as a rule, capable of being presented in a simple metaphor, but we may say that, to the view of the Allied strategy, the huge German salient in the West was like an elastic band drawn very tight. Each part of such a band has lost elasticity, and may be severed by friction which would do little harm to the band if less tautly stretched. That represented one element in the situation. Another aspect might be suggested by the metaphor of a sea-dyke of stone in a flat country where all stone must be imported. The waters crumble the wall in one section, and all free reserves of stone are used to strengthen that part. But the crumbling goes on, and to fill the breach stones are brought from other sections of the dyke. Some day there may come an hour when the sea will wash through the old breach, and a great length of the weakened dyke will follow in the cataclysm.

There were two other motives in the Allied purpose which may be regarded as subsidiary. One was to ease the pressure on Verdun, which during June had grown to fever pitch. The second was to prevent the transference of large bodies of enemy troops from the Western to the Eastern front, a transference which might have worked havoc with Brussilov's plans. Sir Douglas Haig would have preferred to postpone the offensive a little longer, for his numbers and munitionment were still growing, and the training of the new levies was not yet complete. But the general situation demanded that the Allies in the West must not delay their stroke much beyond midsummer.

The German front in the Somme area was held by the right wing of the Second Army, formerly von Buelow's, but now under Otto von Below.* This army's area began just south of Monchy, north of which lay the 6th Army under the Bavarian Crown Prince. At the end of June the front between Gommecourt and Frise was held as follows: North of the Ancre lay the 2nd Guard Reserve Division† and the 52nd Division. Between the Ancre and the Somme lay two units of the 14th Reserve Corps,‡ in order, the 26th Reserve Division, the

---

* His brother, Fritz von Below, was the general commanding the 8th Army on the extreme left of the Eastern front.

† The 2nd Guard Reserve were not true Guardsmen, but only a division used as a reserve for the Guards. The Guards proper were the Guard Corps, comprising the 1st and 2nd Guard Divisions; the Guard Reserve Corps, comprising the 4th Guard Division and the 1st Guard Reserve Division; and the 3rd Guard Division (the "Cockchafers"), who were not classified in any Corps.

‡ The 14th Reserve Corps was a mixed formation, nominally raised in Baden, but containing also Wurtembergers, Prussians, and Alsatians. At the beginning of the campaign it formed part of the 7th Army under von Heeringen which advanced through the northern Vosges. In October

28th Reserve Division, and then the 12th Division of the 6th Reserve Corps. South of the river, guarding the road to Peronne, were the 121st Division, the 11th Division, and the 36th Division, belonging to the 17th (Dantzig) Corps.

The British armies had in less than two years grown from the six divisions of the old Expeditionary Force to a total of some seventy divisions in the field, leaving out of account the troops supplied by the Dominions and by India. Behind these divisions were masses of trained men to replace wastage for at least another year. The quality of the result was not less remarkable than the quantity. The efficiency of the supply and transport, the medical services, the aircraft work, was universally admitted. Our staff and intelligence work—most difficult to improvise—was now equal to the best in the field. Our gunnery was praised by the French, a nation of expert gunners. As for the troops themselves we had secured a homogeneous army of which it was hard to say that one part was better than the other. The original Expeditionary Force—the "Old Contemptibles," who for their numbers were probably the best body of fighting men on earth—had mostly disappeared. Territorial battalions were present at the First Battle of Ypres, and New Service battalions at Hooge and Loos. By June 1916 the term New Armies was a misnomer. The whole British force

1914 it was transferred to the 2nd Army, and since then it had remained in the same section north of the Somme. It comprised the 26th and 28th Reserve Divisions, and the 52nd Division, which was formed early in 1915. It was commanded at the time of the Somme battle by General von Stein.

MACHINE GUN DETAIL EQUIPPED WITH GAS MASKS

in one sense was new. The famous old regiments of the line had been completely renewed since Mons, and their drafts were drawn from the same source as the men of the new battalions. The only difference was that in the historic battalions there was a tradition already existing, whereas in the new battalions that tradition had to be created. And the creation was quick. If the Old Army bore the brunt of the First Battle of Ypres, the Territorials were no less heroic in the Second Battle of Ypres, and the New Army had to its credit the four-mile charge at Loos. It was no patchwork force which in June was drawn up in Picardy, but the flower of the manhood of the British Empire, differing in origin and antecedents, but alike in discipline and courage and resolution.

Munitions had grown with the numbers of men. Any one who was present at Ypres in April and May 1915 saw the German guns all day pounding our lines with only a feeble and intermittent reply. It was better at Loos in September, when we showed that we could achieve an intense bombardment. But at that date our equipment sufficed only for spasmodic efforts and not for that sustained and continuous fire which was needed to destroy the enemy's defences. Things were very different in June 1916. Everywhere on the long British front there were British guns—heavy guns of all calibres, field guns innumerable, and in the trenches there were quantities of trench mortars. The great munition dumps, constantly depleted and constantly replenished from distant bases, showed that there was food and to spare for this mass of artillery, and in the factories and depots at home every minute saw the reserves growing. We no longer fought against a far superior machine. We had created our own machine to nullify the enemy's and allow our man-power to come to grips.

The preparations for the attack were slow and elaborate, and conducted during indifferent weather. Sir Douglas Haig has described them. "Many miles of new railways—both standard and narrow gauge—and trench tramways were laid. All available roads were improved, many others were made, and long causeways were built over marshy valleys. Many additional dug-outs had to be provided as shelter for the troops, for use as dressing stations for the wounded, and as magazines for storing ammunition, food, water, and engineering material. Scores of miles of deep communication trenches had to be dug, as well as trenches for telephone wires, assembly and assault trenches, and numerous gun emplacements and observation posts. Important mining operations were undertaken, and charges were laid at various points beneath the enemy's lines. Except in the river valleys, the existing supplies of water were hopelessly insufficient to meet the requirements of the numbers of men and horses to be concentrated in this area as our preparations for the offensive proceeded. To meet this difficulty many wells and borings were sunk, and over one hundred pumping plants were installed. More than one hundred and twenty miles of water mains were laid, and everything was got ready to ensure an adequate water supply as our troops advanced."

The coming attack was allotted to the Fourth Army, under General Sir Henry Rawlinson, who

had begun the campaign in command of the 7th
Division, and at Loos had commanded the 4th Corps.
His front ran from south of Gommecourt across the
Ancre valley to the junction with the French north
of Maricourt. In his line he had five corps—from
left to right, the 8th, under Lieutenant-General Sir
Aylmer Hunter-Weston; the 10th, under Lieutenant-
General Sir T. L. N. Morland; the 3rd, under Lieutenant-General Sir W. P. Pulteney; the 15th, under
Lieutenant-General Horne; and the 13th, under
Lieutenant-General Congreve, V.C. Behind in the
back areas lay the nucleus of another army, called
first the Reserve, and afterwards the Fifth, under
General Sir Hubert Gough, which at this time was
mainly composed of cavalry divisions. It was a
cadre which would receive its complement of infantry when the occasion arose.

The French striking force lay from Maricourt
astride the Somme to opposite the village of Fay.
It was the Sixth Army, once de Castelnau's, and now
under General Fayolle, one of the most distinguished
of French artillerymen. It comprised the 20th
Corps* of Verdun fame, under General Balfourier;
the 1st Colonial Corps under General Brandelat;
and the 35th Corps under General Allonier. Pétain's

---

* The 20th Corps was composed of the 11th, 39th, and
153rd Divisions. It drew its recruits from the best fighting
stocks of France, the cockneys of Paris and the countrymen
of Lorraine. Each of its divisions claimed to be a "Division
de Fer," but this title was most generally bestowed upon
the 39th. Besides Verdun the 20th Corps had been with
Maud'huy in his great defence of Arras in October 1914, and
in the Artois fighting of the summer of 1915. It was the
153rd Division that mainly turned the tide at Douaumont on
February 26, 1916, and later retook the Avocourt Redoubt.

wise plan of allowing no formation to be used up now received brilliant justification. The divisions allotted to the new offensive were all troops who had seen hard fighting, but the edge of their temper was undulled. To one who visited them in the last days of June it seemed that they awaited the day with a boyish expectancy and glee. South of Fayolle lay the Tenth Army, once d'Urbal's, but now commanded by General Micheler. Its part for the present was to wait; its turn would come when the time arrived to broaden the front of assault.

About the middle of June on the whole ninety-mile front held by the British, and on the French front north and south of the Somme there began an intermittent bombardment of the German lines. There were raids at different places, partly to mislead the enemy as to the real point of assault, and partly to identify the German units opposed to us. Such raids varied widely in method, but they were extraordinarily successful. Sometimes gas was used, but more often after a short bombardment a picked detachment crossed No Man's Land, cut the enemy's wire, and dragged home a score or two of prisoners. One, conducted by a company of the 9th Highland Light Infantry (the Glasgow Highlanders) near the Vermelles-La Bassée Road, deserves special mention. Our guns had damaged the German parapets, so when darkness came a German working-party was put in to mend them. The Scots, while the engineers neatly cut off a section of German trenches, swooped down on the place, investigated the dugouts, killed two score Germans, brought back forty-six prisoners, and had for total casualties two men slightly wounded.* During these days, too, there were many fights in the air. It was essential to prevent German airplanes from crossing our front and observing our preparations. Our own machines scouted far into the enemy hinterland, reconnoitring and destroying.

On Saturday, 24th June, the bombardment became intenser. It fell everywhere on the front; German trenches were obliterated at Ypres and Arras as well as at Beaumont Hamel *June 24.* and Fricourt. There is nothing harder to measure than the relative force of such a "preparation," but had a dispassionate observer been seated in the clouds he would have noted that from Gommecourt to a mile or two south of the Somme the Allied fire was especially methodical and persistent. On Wednesday, 28 June, from an artillery observation post in that region it seemed *June 28.* as if a complete devastation had been achieved. Some things like broken telegraph poles were all that remained of what, a week before, had been leafy copses. Villages had become heaps of rubble. Travelling at night on the roads behind the front— from Bethune to Amiens—the whole eastern sky was lit up with what seemed fitful summer lightning. But there was curiously little noise. In Amiens, a score or so of miles from the firing-line, the guns were rarely heard, whereas fifty miles from Ypres they sounded like a roll of drums and woke a man

* In the week preceding the attack—that is, June 24 to July 1—gas was discharged at more than forty places upon a frontage which in total amounted to over fifteen miles. During the same period some seventy raids were undertaken between Gommecourt and our extreme left north of Ypres.

in the night. The configuration of that part of
Picardy muffles sound, and the country folk call it
the Silent Land.

All the last week of June the weather was grey
and cloudy, with a thick brume on the uplands,
which made air-work unsatisfactory. There were
flying showers of rain and the roads were deep in
mire. At the front—through the haze—the guns
flashed incessantly, and there was that tense expectancy which precedes a great battle. Troops were
everywhere on the move, and the shifting of ammunition dumps nearer to the firing-line fore-
told what was coming. There was a curious exhilaration everywhere. Men felt that the great
offensive had come, that this was no flash in the
pan, but a movement conceived on the grand scale
as to guns and men which would not cease until a
decision was reached. But, as the hours passed in
mist and wet, it seemed as if the fates were unpro-
pitious. Then, on the last afternoon of June, there
June 30.   came a sudden change. The pall of
cloud cleared away and all Picardy swam
in the translucent blue of a summer evening. That
night the orders went out. The attack was to be
delivered next morning three hours after dawn.

The first day of July dawned hot and cloudless, though a thin fog, the relic of the damp of the
July 1.   past week, clung to the hollows. At
half-past five the hill just west of Albert
offered a singular view. It was almost in the centre
of the section allotted to the Allied attack, and from
it the eye could range on the left up and beyond
the Ancre glen to the high ground around Beaumont
Hamel and Serre; in front to the great lift of

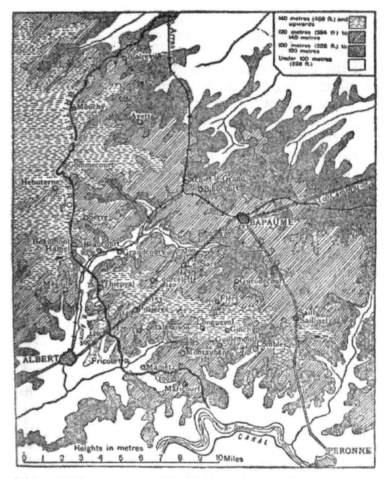

BATTLE OF THE SOMME.—CONTOURED MAP OF THE GROUND ON WHICH THE BRITISH ARMY WAS ENGAGED.

tableland behind which lay Bapaume; and to the
right past the woods of Fricourt to the valley of the
Somme.   Every slope to the east was wreathed in
smoke, which blew aside now and then and revealed
a patch of wood or a church spire.   In the foreground lay Albert, the target of an occasional German shell, with its shattered Church of Notre Dame
de Bebrières and the famous gilt Virgin hanging
head downward from the campanile.   All along the
Allied front, a couple of miles behind the line, captive
kite balloons, the so-called "sausages," glittered in
the sunlight.   Every gun on a front of twenty-five
miles was speaking, and speaking without pause.   In
that week's bombardment more light and medium
ammunition was expended than the total amount
manufactured in Britain during the first eleven
months of war, while the heavy stuff produced during the same period would not have kept our guns
going for a single day.   Great spurts of dust on the
slopes showed where a heavy shell had burst, and
black and white gouts of smoke dotted the middle
distance like the little fires in a French autumn field.
Lace-like shrapnel wreaths hung in the sky, melting
into the morning haze.   The noise was strangely
uniform, a steady rumbling, as if the solid earth
were muttering in a nightmare, and it was hard to
distinguish the deep tones of the heavies, the vicious
whip-like crack of the field guns and the bark of the
trench mortars.

About 7.15 the bombardment rose to that hurricane pitch of fury which betokened its close.   It was
as if titanic machine guns were at work round all
the horizon.   Then appeared a marvellous sight,
the solid spouting of the enemy slopes—as if they

were lines of reefs on which a strong tide was breaking. In such a hell it seemed that no human thing could live. Through the thin summer vapour and the thicker smoke which clung to the foreground there were visions of a countryside actually moving —moving bodily in débris into the air. And now there was a fresh sound—a series of abrupt and rapid bursts which came gustily from the first lines. These were the new trench mortars—wonderful little engines of death. There was another sound, too, from the north, as if the cannonading had suddenly come nearer. It looked as if the Germans had begun a counter-bombardment on part of the British front line.

The staff officers glanced at their watches, and at half-past seven precisely there came a lull. It lasted for a second or two, and then the guns continued their tale. But the range had been lengthened everywhere, and from a bombardment the fire had become a *barrage*. For, on a twenty-five mile front, the Allied infantry had gone over the parapets.

CHAPTER II

THE FIRST STAGE

THE point of view of the hill-top was not that of the men in the front trenches. The crossing of the parapets is the supreme moment in modern war. The troops are outside defences, moving across the open to investigate the unknown. It is the culmination of months of training for officers and men, and the least sensitive feels the drama of the crisis. Most of the British troops engaged had twenty months before been employed in peaceable civilian trades. In their ranks were every class and condition—miners from north England, factory hands from the industrial centres, clerks and shopboys, ploughmen and shepherds, Saxon and Celt, college graduates and dock labourers, men who in the wild places of the earth had often faced danger, and men whose chief adventure had been

34

a Sunday bicycle ride. Nerves may be attuned to
the normal risks of trench warfare and yet shrink
from the desperate hazard of a charge into the
enemy's line.

But to one who visited the front before the
attack the most vivid impression was that of quiet
cheerfulness. There were no shirkers and few who
wished themselves elsewhere. One man's imagina-
tion might be more active than another's, but the
will to fight, and to fight desperately, was universal.
With the happy gift of the British soldier they had
turned the ghastly business of war into something
homely and familiar. Accordingly they took everything as part of the day's work, and awaited the
supreme moment without heroics and without
tremor, confident in themselves, confident in their
guns, and confident in the triumph of their cause.
There was no savage lust of battle, but that far more
formidable thing—a resolution which needed no
rhetoric to support it. Norfolk's words were true
of every man of them:

"As gentle and as jocund as to jest
Go I to fight. Truth hath a quiet breast." *

* A letter written before the action by a young officer
gives expression to this joyful resolution. He fell in the
first day's battle and the letter was posted after his death :—
"I am writing this letter to you just before going into
action to-morrow morning about dawn.
"I am about to take part in the biggest battle that has
yet been fought in France, and one which ought to help to
end the war very quickly.
"I never felt more confident or cheerful in my life before,
and would not miss the attack for anything on earth. The
men are in splendid form, and every officer and man is more
happy and cheerful than I have ever seen them. I have

The British aim in this, the opening stage of the
battle, was the German first position. The attached
map shows its general line. In the section of assault,
running from north to south, it covered Gommecourt, passed east of Hebuterne, followed the high
ground in front of Serre and Beaumont Hamel, and
crossed the Ancre a little to the north-west of Thiepval. It ran in front of Thiepval, which was very
strongly fortified, east of Authuille, and just covered
the hamlets of Ovillers and La Boisselle. There it
ran about a mile and a quarter east of Albert. It
then passed south round the woodland village of

just been playing a rag game of football in which the umpire
had a revolver and a whistle.

"My idea in writing this letter is in case I am one of the
'costs,' and get killed. I do not expect to be, but such things
have happened, and are always possible.

"It is impossible to fear death out here when one is no
longer an individual, but a member of a regiment and of an
army. To be killed means nothing to me, and it is only you
who suffer for it; you really pay the cost.

"I have been looking at the stars, and thinking what an
immense distance they are away. What an insignificant
thing the loss of, say, 40 years of life is compared with them!
It seems scarcely worth talking about.

"Well, good-bye, you darlings. Try not to worry about
it, and remember that we shall meet again really quite soon.

"This letter is going to be posted if . . . Lots of love.
From your loving son,

> "Qui procul hinc
> Ante diem periit,
> Sed miles, sed pro Patria."

Fricourt, where it turned at right angles to the east,
covering Mametz and Montauban. Half-way between Maricourt and Hardecourt it turned south

DISTRIBUTION OF AMMUNITION TO MEN RETURNING TO FIRE TRENCH

A ROLL-CALL ON THE AFTERNOON OF JULY FIRST

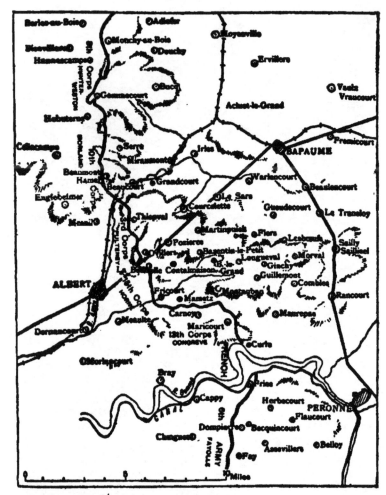

BATTLE OF THE SOMME.—THE FRONT FROM MONCHY TO FAY, JULY IST
(SHOWING GENERAL ARRANGEMENT OF THE OPPOSING ARMIES).

again, covered Curlu, crossed the Somme at the wide marsh near the place called Vaux, covered Frise and Dompierre and Soyecourt, and passed just east of Lihons, where it left the sector with which we are now concerned.

The British front of attack* was disposed as follows: From opposite Gommecourt to just south of Beaumont Hamel lay the right wing of Sir Edmund Allenby's Third Army and General Hunter Weston's 8th Corps. From just north of the Ancre to Authuille was General Morland's 10th Corps, East of Albert lay General Pulteney's 3rd Corps, one division being directed against Ovillers, and another against La Boisselle. South, curving round the Fricourt salient to Mametz, lay General Horne's 15th Corps. On the British right flank adjoining the French lay General Congreve's 13th Corps.

It is clear that the Germans expected the attack of the Allies, and had made a fairly accurate guess as to its *terrain*. They assumed that the area would be from Arras to Albert. In all that area they were ready with a full concentration of men and guns. South of Albert they were less prepared, and south of the Somme they were caught napping. The history of the first day is therefore the story of two separate actions in the north and south, in the first of which the Allies failed and in the second of which they brilliantly succeeded. By the evening the first action had definitely closed, and the weight of the Allies was flung wholly into the second. That is almost inevitable in an attack on a very broad front.

* According to the official dispatch the main British front of attack was intended to be from Maricourt to the Ancre. The attack from the Ancre to Gommecourt was subsidiary.

Some part will be found tougher than the rest, and that part having been tried will be relinquished; but it is the stubbornness of the knot and the failure to take it which are the price of success elsewhere. Let us first tell the tale of the desperate struggle between Gommecourt and Thiepval.

The divisions in action there were three from the New Army, two of the old regulars, which had won fame both in Flanders and Gallipoli, and one Territorial brigade. They had to face a chain of fortified villages—Gommecourt, Serre, Beaumont Hamel, and Thiepval—and enemy positions which were generally on higher and better ground. The Ancre cut the line in two, with steep slopes rising from the valley bottom. Each village had been so fortified as to be almost impregnable, with a maze of catacombs, often two stories deep, where whole battalions could take refuge, underground passages from the firing-line to sheltered places in the rear, and pits into which machine guns could be lowered during a bombardment. On the plateau behind, with excellent direct observation, the Germans had their guns massed.

It was this direct observation and the deep shelters for machine guns which were the undoing of the British attack from Gommecourt *July* 1. to Thiepval. As our bombardment grew more intense on the morning of 1st July, so did the enemy's. Before our men could go over the parapets the Germans had plastered our front trenches with high explosives, and in many places blotted them out. All along our line, fifty yards before and behind the first trench, they dropped 6-inch and

8-inch high-explosive shells.   The result was that
our men, instead of forming up in the front trench,
were compelled to form up in the open ground
behind, for the front trench had disappeared.   In
addition to this there was an intense shrapnel *barrage,* which must have been directed by observers,
for it followed our troops as they moved forward.

At Beaumont Hamel, under the place called
Hawthorn Redoubt, we had constructed a mine, the
largest yet known in the campaign.   At 7.30 acres
of land leaped into the air, and our men advanced
under the shadow of a pall of dust which turned
the morning into twilight.   "The exploding cham-
ber," said a sergeant, describing it afterwards, "was
as big as a picture palace, and the gallery was an
awful length.   It took us seven months to build,
and we were working under some of the crack Lan-
cashire miners.   Every time a fresh fatigue party
came up they'd say to the miners, 'Ain't your grotto
ever going up?'   But, my lord! it went up all
right on 1st July.   It was the sight of your life.
Half the village got a rise.   The air was full of
stuff—wagons, wheels, horses, tins, boxes, and
Germans.   It was seven months well spent getting
that mine ready.   I believe some of the pieces are
coming down still."

As our men began to cross No Man's Land, the
Germans seemed to man their ruined parapets, and
fired rapidly with automatic rifles and machine guns.
They had special light *musketon* battalions, armed
with machine guns and automatic rifles, who showed
marvellous intrepidity, some even pushing their guns
forward into No Man's Land to enfilade our advance.   Moreover they had machine-gun pits far

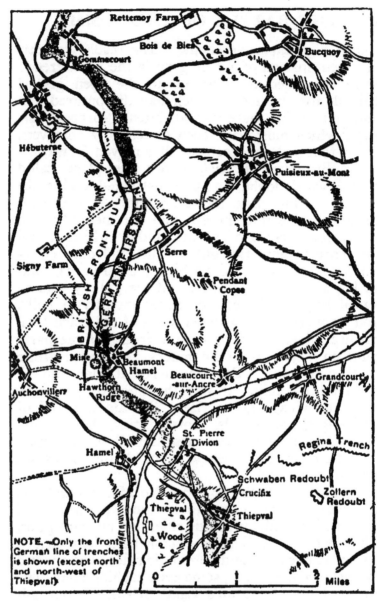

BATTLE OF THE SOMME.—FRONT OF BRITISH LEFT ATTACK, JULY (GOMME-
COURT TO THIEPVAL).

in front of their parapets, connected with the
trenches by deep tunnels secure from shell-fire
The British moved forward in line after line, dresse
as if on parade; not a man wavered or broke rank
but minute by minute the ordered lines melted awa
under the deluge of high-explosive, shrapnel, rifle
and machine-gun fire. There was no question abou
the German weight of artillery. From dawn till long
after noon they maintained this steady drenching
fire. Gallant individuals or isolated detachment
managed here and there to break into the enemy
position, and some even penetrated well behind it
but these were episodes, and the ground they wor
could not be held. By the evening, from Gommecourt to Thiepval, the attack had been everywhere
checked, and our troops—what was left of them—
were back again in their old line. They had struck
the core of the main German defence.

In that stubborn action against impossible odds
the gallantry was so universal and absolute that it
is idle to select special cases. In each mile there
were men who performed the incredible. Nearly
every English, Scots, and Irish regiment was represented, as well as Midland and London Territorials,
a gallant little company of Rhodesians, and a New-
foundland battalion drawn from the hard-bitten
fishermen of that iron coast, who lost terribly on
the slopes of Beaumont Hamel. Repeatedly the
German position was pierced. At Serre fragments
of two battalions pushed as far as Pendant Copse,
2,000 yards from the British lines. Troops of one
division broke through south of Beaumont Hamel,
and got to the Station Road beyond the Quarry,
but few ever returned. One Scottish battalion en-

tered Thiepval village. North of Thiepval the
Ulster Division broke through the enemy trenches,
passed the crest of the ridge, and reached the point
called The Crucifix, in rear of the first German
position. For a little they held the strong Schwaben
Redoubt, which we were not to enter again till after
three months of battle, and some even got into the
outskirts of Grandcourt. It was the anniversary day
of the Battle of the Boyne, and that charge when the
men shouted "Remember the Boyne" will be for
ever a glorious page in the annals of Ireland. The
Royal Irish Fusiliers were first out of the trenches.
The Royal Irish Rifles followed them over the German parapets, bayoneting the machine gunners, and
the Inniskillings cleared the trenches to which they
had given Irish names. Enfiladed on three sides they
went on through successive German lines, and only
a remnant came back to tell the tale. That remnant brought many prisoners, one man herding fifteen of the enemy through their own *barrage*. In
the words of the general who commanded it: "The
division carried out every portion of its allotted task
in spite of the heaviest losses. It captured nearly
600 prisoners and carried its advance triumphantly
to the limits of the objective laid down." Nothing
finer was done in the war. The splendid troops,
drawn from those volunteers who had banded themselves together for another cause, now shed their
blood like water for the liberty of the world.

That grim struggle from Thiepval northward
was responsible for by far the greater number of
the Allied losses of the day. But, though costly, it
was not fruitless, for it occupied the bulk of the
German defence. It was the price which had to be

paid for the advance of the rest of the front. For, while in the north the living wave broke vainly and gained little, in the south "by creeks and inlets making" the tide was flowing strongly shoreward.

The map will show that Fricourt forms a bold salient; and it was the Allied purpose not to assault this salient but to cut it off. An advance on Ovillers and La Boisselle and up the long shallow depression towards Contalmaison, which our men called Sausage Valley, would, if united with the carrying of Mametz, pinch it so tightly that it must fall. Ovillers and La Boisselle were strongly fortified villages, and on this first day, while we won the outskirts and carried the entrenchments before them, we did not control the ruins which our guns had pounded out of the shape of habitable dwellings. Elements of one brigade actually penetrated into La Boisselle, and held a portion of the village.

Just west of Fricourt a division was engaged which had suffered grave misfortunes at Loos. That day it got back its own, and proved once again that an enemy can meet no more formidable foes than British troops which have a score to wipe off. It made no mistake, but poured resolutely into the angle east of Sausage Valley, carrying Lozenge Wood and Round Wood, and driving in a deep wedge north of Fricourt.

Before evening Mametz fell. Its church stood up, a broken tooth of masonry among the shattered houses, with an amphitheatre of splintered woods behind and around it. South of it ran a high road, and south of the road lay a little hill, with the German trench lines on the southern side. Opposite

ARTILLERY OBSERVATION POST IN REAR OF GERMAN LINE

CLEARING A ROAD THROUGH CONTALMAISON

Mametz our assembly trenches had been destroyed by the enemy's fire, so that the attacking infantry had to advance over 400 yards of open ground. The division which took the place was one of the most renowned in the British Army. It had fought at First Ypres, at Festubert, and at Loos. Since the autumn of 1914 it had been changed in its composition, but there were in it battalions which had been for twenty months in the field. The whole division, old and new alike, went forward to their task as if it were the first day of war. On the slopes of the little hill three battalions advanced in line—one from a southern English county, one from a northern city, one of Highland regulars. They carried everything before them, and to one who followed their track the regularity of their advance was astonishing, for the dead lay aligned as if on some parade.

Montauban fell early in the day, the Manchesters being the first troops to enter. The British lines lay in the hollow north of the Albert-Peronne road, where stands the hamlet of Carnoy. On the crest of the ridge beyond lay Montauban, now, like most Santerre villages, a few broken walls set among splintered trees. The brickfields on the right were expected to be the scene of a fierce struggle, but, to our amazement, they had been so shattered by our guns that they were taken easily. The Montauban attack was perhaps the most perfect of the episodes of the day. The artillery had done its work, and the 6th Bavarian Regiment opposed to us lost 3,000 out of a total strength of 3,500. The division which formed the British right wing moved forward in parade order to a speedy success.

At that point was seen a sight hitherto unwitnessed in the campaign—the advance in line of the troops of Britain and France. On the British right lay the 20th Corps—the corps which had held the Grand Couronné of Nancy in the feverish days of the Marne battle, and which by its counter-attack at Douaumont on that snowy 26th of February had turned the tide at Verdun. It was the 39th Division, under General Nourrisson, which moved in line with the British—horizon-blue beside khaki, and behind both the comforting bark of the incomparable "75's."

To walk over the captured ground was to learn a profound respect for the beaver-like industry of the German soldier. His fatigue-work must have reached the heroic scale. The old firing trenches were so badly smashed by our guns that it was hard to follow them, but what was left was good. The soil of the place was the best conceivable for digging, for it cut like cheese, and hardened like brick in dry weather. The map shows a ramification of little red lines, but only the actual sight of that labyrinth could give a true impression of its strength. One communication trench, for example, was a tunnel a hundred yards long, lined with timber throughout, and so deep as to be beyond the reach of the heaviest shells. The small manholes used for snipers' posts were skilfully contrived. Tunnels led to them from the trenches, and the openings were artfully screened by casual-looking débris. But the greatest marvels were the dug-outs. One at Fricourt had nine rooms and five bolt-holes; it had iron doors, gas curtains, linoleum on the floors, wallpaper and pictures on the walls, and boasted a good bath-room, electric light, and electric bells. The staff which occupied it must have lived in luxury. Many of these dug-outs had two storeys, a thirty foot staircase, beautifully finished, leading to the first suite, and a second stair of the same length conducting to a lower storey. In such places machine guns could be protected during any bombardment. But the elaboration of such dwellings went far beyond military needs. When the Germans boasted that their front on the West was impregnable they sincerely believed it. They thought they had established a continuing city, from which they would emerge only at a triumphant peace. The crumbling—not of their front trenches only but of their whole first position—was such a shock as King Priam's court must have received when the Wooden Horse disgorged the Greeks in the heart of their citadel.

It was not won without stark fighting. The British soldiers were quick to kindle in the fight, and more formidable figures than those bronzed, steel-hatted warriors history has never seen on a field of battle. Those who witnessed the charge of the Highlanders at Loos were not likely to forget its fierce resolution. Said a French officer who was present: "I don't know what effect it had on the Boche, but it made *my* blood run cold." Our men were fighting against the foes of humanity, and they did not make war as a joke. But there was none of the savagery which comes either from a half-witted militarism or from rattled nerves. The Germans had been officially told that the British took no prisoners, and this falsehood, while it made the stouter fellows fight to the death, sent scores of poor creatures huddling in dug-outs, from which they had to be extracted like shell-fish. But, after surrender, there was no brutality—very much the reverse. As one watched the long line of wounded —the "walking cases"—straggling back from the firing-line to a dressing-station, they might have been all of one side. One picture remains in the memory. Two wounded Gordon Highlanders were hobbling along, and supported between them a wounded Badener. The last seen of the trio was that the Scots were giving him water and cigarettes, and he was cutting buttons from his tunic as souvenirs for his comforters. A letter of an officer on this point is worth quoting:—

"The more I see of war the more I am convinced of the fundamental decency of our own folk. They may have a crude taste in music and art and things of that sort; they may lack the patient industry of the Boche; but for sheer goodness of heart, for kindness to all unfortunate things, like prisoners, wounded, animals, and ugly women, they fairly beat the band."

It is the kind of tribute which most Britons would prefer to any other.

From the point of junction with the British for eight miles southward the French advanced with lightning speed and complete success. From Maricourt to the Somme the country was still upland, but lower than the region to the north. South of the marshy Somme valley an undulating plain stretched east to the great crook of the river beyond which lay Peronne, a fortress girdled by its moat of three streams. General Foch had planned his advance on the same lines as the British, the same methodical preparation, the same limited objective

for each stage. North of the Somme, where Balfourier had to face the 10th Bavarians and the 12th
Division, there was a stiff fight on the Albert-Peronne road, at the cliff abutting on the river called
the "Gendarme's Hat," and in front of the villages
of Curlu and Hardecourt. Of these on that 1st day
of July the French reached the outskirts, as we
reached the outskirts of Fricourt and La Boisselle,
but had to postpone their capture till the morrow.
South of the river the Colonials, whose attack did
not begin till 9.30 a.m., took the enemy completely
by surprise. Officers were captured shaving in their
dug-outs, whole battalions were rounded up, and all
was done with the minimum of loss. One French
regiment had two casualties; 800 was the total of
one division. Long ere the evening the villages of
Dompierre, Becquincourt, and Bussu were in their
hands, and five miles had been bitten out of the
German front. Fay was taken the same day by the
Bretons of the 35th Corps. Between them the Allies
that day had captured the enemy first position in
its entirety from Mametz to Fay, a front of fourteen miles. Some six thousand prisoners were in
their hands, and a great quantity of guns and stores.
In the powdered trenches, in the woods and valleys
behind, and in the labyrinths of ruined dwellings,
the German dead lay thick. "That is the purpose
of the battle," said a French officer. "We do not
want guns, for Krupp can make them faster than
we can take them. But Krupp cannot make
men."

Sunday, the 2nd of July, was a day of level
heat, when the dust stood in steady walls on every
road behind the front and in the tortured areas of

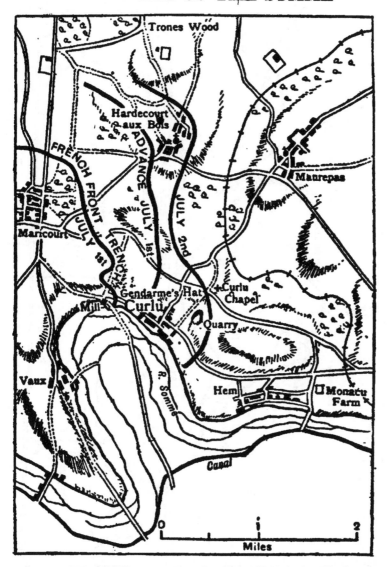

BATTLE OF THE SOMME.—THE FIRST FRENCH ADVANCE NORTH OF THE
SOMME.

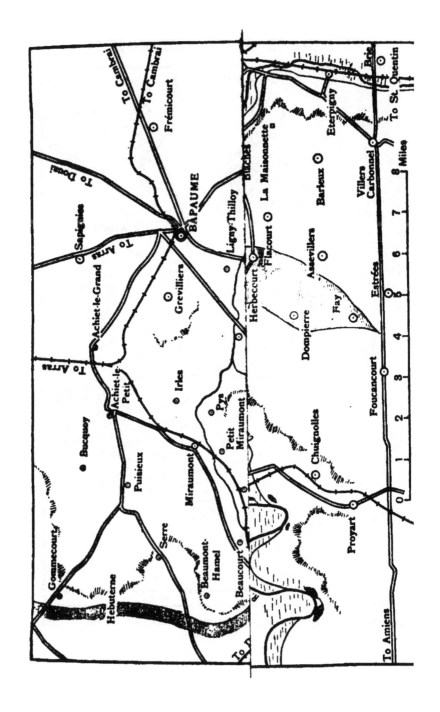

the captured ground. The success of the Saturday had, as we have seen, put the British right wing well in advance of their centre, and it was necessary to bring forward the left part of the line from Thiepval to Fricourt so as *July 2.* to make the breach in the German position uniform over a broad enough front. The extreme British left was now inactive. A new attack in the circumstances would have given no results, and the Ulster Division—what remained of its advanced guard—fell back from the Schwaben Redoubt to its original line. The front was rapidly getting too large and intricate for any single army commander to handle, so it was resolved to give the *terrain* north of the Albert-Bapaume road, including the area of the 4th and 8th Corps, to the Reserve or Fifth Army, under Sir Hubert Gough.

All that day a fierce struggle was waged by the 3rd Corps at Ovillers and La Boisselle. Two new divisions had entered the line. At Ovillers one of them carried the entrenchments before it, and late in the evening the other succeeded in entering the labyrinth of cellars, the ruins of what had been La Boisselle. The troops on their right, pushing across Sausage Valley, came to the skirts of the Round Wood. As yet there was no counter-attack. The surprise in the south had been too great, and the Germans had not yet brought up their reserve divisions. All that day squadrons of Allied airplanes bombed depots and lines of communications in the German hinterland. The long echelons of the Allied "sausages" glittered in the sun, but only one German kite balloon could be detected. We had found a way—the Verdun way—of bombing those fragile gas-bags and turning them into wisps of flame. The Fokkers strove in vain to check our airmen, and at least two were brought crashing to the earth.

At noon on Sunday Fricourt fell; the taking of Mametz and the positions won in the Fricourt Wood to the east had made its capture certain. One division took Round Wood; a second, brought up from corps reserve, attacked across the Fricourt-Contalmaison road; and a third carried the village. During the night part of the garrison had slipped out, but when our men entered it, bombing from house to house, they made a great haul of prisoners and guns. Early that morning the Germans had counter-attacked at Montauban, and been easily repulsed, and during the day our patrols were pushed east into Bernafay Wood.

Farther south the French continued their victorious progress. They destroyed a German counter-attack on the new position at Hardecourt; they took Curlu; and, south of the river, they took Frise and the wood of Méreaucourt beyond it, and the strongly fortified village of Herbecourt. They did more, for at many points between the river and Assevilliers they broke into the German second position. Fayolle's left now commanded the light railway from Combles to Peronne, his centre held the big loop of the Somme at Frise, and his right was only four miles from Peronne itself.

On Monday, 3rd July, General von Below issued an order to his troops, which showed that, whatever *July 3.* official Germany might say, the German soldiers had no delusion as to the gravity of the Allied offensive.

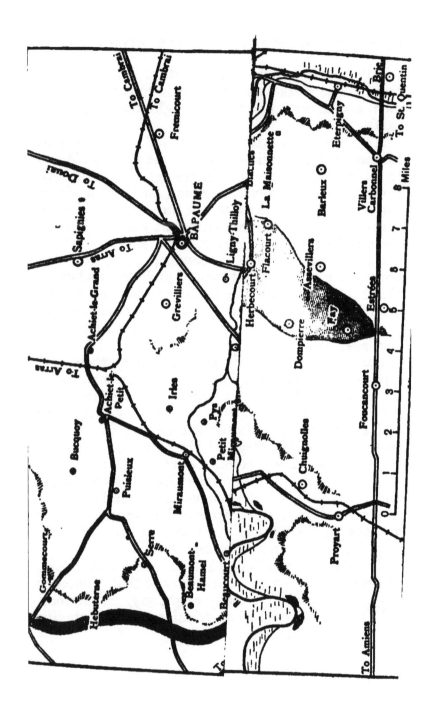

K   L

"The decisive issue of the war depends on the victory of the 2nd Army on the Somme. We must win this battle in spite of the enemy's temporary superiority in artillery and infantry. The important ground lost in certain places will be recaptured by our attack after the arrival of reinforcements. The vital thing is to hold on to our present positions at all costs and to improve them. I forbid the voluntary evacuation of trenches. The will to stand firm must be impressed on every man in the army. The enemy should have to carve his way over heaps of corpses. . . . I require commanding officers to devote their utmost energies to the establishment of order behind the front."

Von Below had correctly estimated the position. The old ground, with all it held, must be re-won if possible; no more must be lost; fresh lines must be constructed in the rear. But the new improvised lines could be no equivalent of those mighty fastnesses which represented the work of eighteen months. Therefore those fastnesses must be regained. We shall learn how ill his enterprise prospered.

For a correct understanding of the position on Monday, 3rd July, it is necessary to recall the exact alignment of the new British front. It fell into two sections. The first lay from Thiepval to Fricourt, and was bisected by the Albert-Bapaume road, which ran like an arrow over the watershed. Here Thiepval, Ovillers, and La Boisselle were positions in the German first line. Contalmaison, to the east of La Boisselle, was a strongly fortified village on high ground, which formed, so to speak, a pivot in the German intermediate line—the line which covered their field guns. The second position ran through Pozières to the two Bazentins and on to Guillemont. On the morning of 3rd July the British had not got

Thiepval, nor Ovillers; they had only a portion of La Boisselle; but south of it they had broken through the first position and were well on the road to Contalmaison. All this northern section consisted of bare undulating slopes—once covered with crops, but now powdered and bare like some alkali desert. Everywhere it was seamed with the scars of trenches and pock-marked with shell holes. The few trees lining the roads had been long razed, and the only vegetation was coarse grass, thistles, and the ubiquitous poppy and mustard.

The southern section, from Fricourt to Montauban, was of a different character. It was patched with large woods, curiously clean cut like the copses in the park of a country house. A line of them ran from Fricourt north-eastward—Fricourt Wood, Bottom Wood, the big wood of Mametz, the woods of Bazentin, and the wood of Foureaux, which our men called High Wood; while from Montauban ran a second line, the woods of Bernafay and Trônes and Delville Wood around Longueval. Here all the German first position had been captured. The second position ran through the Bazentins, Longueval, and Guillemont, but to reach it some difficult woodland country had to be traversed. On 3rd July, therefore, the southern half of the British line was advancing against the enemy's second position, while the northern half had still for its objective Ovillers and La Boisselle in the first position and the intermediate point, Contalmaison.

It will be convenient to take the two sections separately, since their problems were different, and see the progress of the British advance in each, preparatory to the assault on the enemy's second posi-

tion.   In the north our task was to carry the three
fortified places, Ovillers, La Boisselle, and Contalmaison, which were on a large scale the equivalent
of the *fortins,* manned by machine guns, which we
had known to our cost at Festubert and Loos.
Thiepval on the extreme left was less important, for
the high ground could be won without its capture.
The German troops in this area obeyed to the full
von Below's instructions and fought hard for every
acre.   On the night of Sunday, 2nd July, La Boisselle was penetrated, and all Monday the struggle
swayed around that village and Ovillers.   La Boisselle lies on the right of the high road; Ovillers is
to the north and a little to the east, separated by
a dry hollow which we called Mash Valley.   On
Monday one division attacked south of Thiepval,
but failed to advance, largely because its left flank
was unsupported.   All night the struggle see-sawed,
our troops winning ground and the Germans winning back small portions.   On Tuesday, *July 4.*
the 4th, the heat wave broke in thunderstorms and torrential rain, and the dusty hollows
became quagmires. Next morning La Boisselle was
finally carried, after one of the bloodiest contests of
the battle, and the attack was carried forwards toward Bailiff Wood and Contalmaison.

That day, Wednesday, the 5th, we attacked the
Horseshoe Trench, the main defence of Contalmaison from the west.   There a West *July 5.*
Yorks battalion distinguished themselves
by a bold advance.   On Friday, 7th July, came
the first big attack on Contalmaison from Sausage
Valley on the south-west, and from the tangle of
copses north-east of Fricourt, through which ran

the Fricourt-Contalmaison high road. On the latter
side good work had already been done, the enemy
fortins at Birch Tree Wood and Shelter Wood and
the work called the Quadrangle having been taken
on 3rd July, along with 1,100 prisoners.   On the
July 7.   Friday the attack ranged from the Leipzig Redoubt, south of Thiepval, and the
environs of Ovillers to the skirts of Contalmaison.
About noon our infantry, after carrying Bailiff
Wood, took Contalmaison by storm, releasing a small
party of Northumberland Fusiliers, who had been
made prisoners four days earlier.   The 3rd Prussian
Guard Division—the famous "Cockchafers"—were
now our opponents.   They were heavily punished,
and 700 of them fell as prisoners into our hands.   But
our success at Contalmaison was beyond our strength
to maintain, and in the afternoon a counter-attack
forced us out of the village.   That same day our left
wing had pushed their front nearly half a mile along
the Bapaume road, east of La Boisselle, and taken
most of the Leipzig Redoubt.   Ovillers was now in
danger of envelopment.   One brigade had attacked
in front, and another, pressing in on the north-east
flank, was cutting the position in two.   All that day
there was a deluge of rain, and the sodden ground
and flooded trenches crippled the movement of our
men.

Next day the struggle for Ovillers continued.   The
place was now a mass of battered trenches, rub-
July 8.   ble, and muddy shell-holes, and every
yard had to be fought for.   We were also
slowly consolidating our ground around Contalmaison, and driving the Germans from their strongholds in the little copses.   Ever since 7th July we

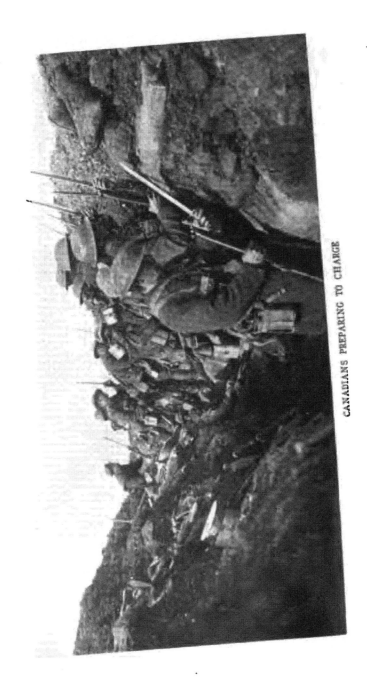

CANADIANS PREPARING TO CHARGE

had held the southern corner of the village. On
the night of Monday, the 10th, pushing
from Bailiff Wood on the west side in
July 10.
four successive waves, with the guns lifting the
range in front of us, we broke into the north-west
corner, swept round on the north, and after bitter
hand-to-hand fighting conquered the whole village.
As for Ovillers, it was now surrounded and beyond
succour, and it was only a question of days till its
stubborn garrison must yield. It did not actually fall
till Sunday, 16th July, when the gallant
remnant—two officers and 124 Guards-
July 16.
men—surrendered. By that time our main push had
swept far to the eastward.

A good description of the country over which we
had advanced is contained in a letter of an officer
to a friend who had been invalided home:—

"I suppose it would seem nothing to other people, but
you, who were here with us through all those dismal winter
months, will understand how thrilling it was to be able to
walk about on that ground in broad daylight, smoking one's
pipe. You remember how our chaps used to risk their lives
in the early days for such silly souvenirs as nose-caps and that
kind of thing. You could gather them by the cartload now,
and Boche caps and buttons, and bits of uniform and boots,
and broken rifles and odd tags of equipment—cartloads of it.
To other folk, and on the maps, one place seems just like
another, I suppose; but to us—La Boisselle and Ovillers—my
hat! To walk about in those hells! Not one of those broken
walls we knew so well (through our glasses) is standing now;
and only a few jagged spikes where the trees were. I went
along the 'sunken road' all the way to Contalmaison. Talk
about sacred ground. When I think what that No Man's
Land was to us for nearly a year! The new troops coming
up now go barging across it in the most light-hearted way.
They know nothing about it. It means no more to them
than the roads behind used to mean to us. It's all behind,

to them, and never was the front. But when I think ht
watered every yard of it with blood and sweat! Ch
might play there now, if it didn't look so much like the
math of an earthquake. But you know there's a kind
wrench about seeing the new chaps swagger over it so
lessly, and seeing it gradually merged into the 'behin
line' country. I have a sort of feeling it ought to be m
off somehow, a permanent memorial.

"You remember that old couple who had the blacksn
shop at ——. The wife was down at the corner by
the other night, when I came along with half the pla
I found her wringing the hands of some of our stolid c
and couldn't make it out. Then she told me, half sob
how she and her husband owned a couple of fields just be
our old front line, and how she wanted to thank us for ge
them back. Think what those fields must have been in
spring of 1914, and what they are to-day, every yard
them torn by shells, burrowed through and through by
trenches and dug-outs; think of the hundreds of tons
wire, sand-bags, timber, galvanised iron, duck-boards,
vetting stuff, steel, iron, blood and sweat, the rum jars, bu
beef tins, old trench boots, field dressings, cartridge cas
rockets, wire stanchions and stakes, gas gongs, bomb boxt
S.A.A. cases, broken canteens, bits of uniforms, and burit
soldiers, and Boches—all in the old lady's two little field
Think how she must have felt, after two years, to know we
got them back. She's walked over them by now, I daresay.

To turn to the southern sector, where the prob
lem was to clear out the fortified woods which in
tervened between us and the German second line
From the crest of the first ridge behind Fricourt and
Montauban one looks into a shallow trough, called
Caterpillar Valley, beyond which the ground rises
to the Bazentin-Longueval line. On the left, toward
Contalmaison, is the big Mametz Wood; to the right,
beyond Montauban, the pear-shaped woods of Bernafay and Trônes.

On Monday, the 3rd, the ground east of Fricourt

Wood was cleared, and the approaches to Mametz Wood won. That day a German counter-attack developed. A fresh division ar- July 3. rived at Montauban, which was faithfully handled by our guns. The "milking of the line" had begun, for a battalion from the Champagne front appeared east of Mametz early on Monday morning. With-in a very short time of detraining at railhead the whole battalion had been destroyed or made pris-oners. In one small area over a thousand men were taken. A wounded officer of a Highland regiment has described the scene:—

"It was the finest show I ever saw in my life. There were six hundred Boches of all ranks marching in column of route across the open back towards our rear. They were disarmed, of course. And what do you think they had for escort? Three ragged Jocks of our battalion, all blood and dirt and rags, with their rifles at the slope, doing a sort of G.O.C.'s inspection parade march, like pipers at the head of a battalion. That was good enough for me. I brought up the rear, and that's how I got to a dressing-station and had my arm dressed. I walked behind a six hundred strong column of Boches, but I couldn't equal the swagger of those three Jocks in the lead."

Next day, Tuesday, 4th July, we had entered the Wood of Mametz, 3,000 yards north of Mametz village, and had taken the Wood of Ber- July 4. nafay. These intermediate positions were not acquired without a grim struggle. The woods were thick with undergrowth which had not been cut for two seasons, and though our artillery played havoc with the trees it could not clear away the tangled shrubbery beneath them. The Ger-mans had filled the place with machine-gun re-doubts, connected by concealed trenches, and in some cases they had machine guns in positions in the trees. Each step in our advance had to be fought for, and in that briery labyrinth the battle tended always to become a series of individual combats. Every position we won was subjected at once to a heavy counter-bombardment. During the first two days of July it was possible to move in moderate safety almost up to the British firing-lines, but from the 4th onward the enemy kept up a steady bombardment of our whole new front, and *barraged* heavily in all the hinterland around Fricourt, Mametz, and Montauban.

On Saturday, 8th July, we made a lodgment in the Wood of Trônes, assisted by the flanking fire *July 8.* of the French guns. On that day the French on our right were advancing towards Maltzhorn Farm. For the next five days Trônes Wood was the hottest corner in the southern British sector. Its peculiar situation gave every chance to the defence. There was only one covered approach to it from the west—by way of the trench called Trônes Alley. The southern part was commanded by the Maltzhorn ridge, and the northern by the German position at Longueval. Around the wood to north and east the enemy second line lay in a half-moon, so that they could concentrate upon it a converging artillery fire, and could feed their own garrison in the place with reserves at their pleasure. Finally, the denseness of the covert, cut only by the railway clearings and the German communication trenches, made organised movement impossible. It was not till our pressure elsewhere diverted the German artillery fire that the wood as a whole could be won. Slowly and stub-

bornly we pushed our way northwards from our
point of lodgment in the southern end.   Six counter-
attacks were launched against us on Sunday night

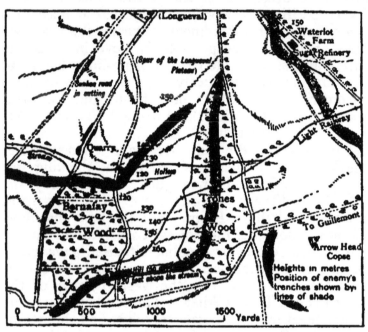

BATTLE OF THE SOMME.—BERNAFAY AND TRONES WOODS.

and Monday, and on Monday afternoon the sixth
succeeded in winning back some of the   *July* 10.
wood. These desperate efforts exactly
suited our purpose, for the German losses under our
artillery fire were enormous. The fighting was continued on Tuesday, when we recaptured the whole
of the wood except the extreme northern   *July* 11.
corner. That same day we approached
the north end of Mametz Wood.   The difficulty of

the fighting and the strength of the defence may
be realised from the fact that the taking of a few
hundred yards or so of woodland meant invariably
the capture of several hundred prisoners.

' By Wednesday evening, 12th July, we had taken
virtually the whole of Mametz Wood. Its two hundred odd acres, interlaced with barbed
July 12.   wire, honeycombed with trenches, and
bristling with machine guns, had given us a tough
struggle, especially the last strip on the north side,
where the German machine-gun positions enfiladed
every advance. Next day we cleared this corner and
broke out of the wood, and were face to face at last
with the main German second position.   Meantime,
the Wood of Trônes had become a Tom Tiddler's
Ground, which neither antagonist could fully claim
or use as a base.   It was at the mercy· of the artillery fire of both sides, and it was impossible in
the time to construct shell-proof defences.

In the French section the advance had been swift
and continuous.   The attack, as we have seen,
was a complete surprise; for, half an hour before
it began on 1st July, an order was issued to
the German troops, predicting the imminent fall of
Verdun, and announcing that a French offensive
elsewhere had thereby been prevented.   On the
nine-mile front from Maricourt to Estrées the
German first position had been carried the first
day. The heavy guns, when they had sufficiently
pounded it, ceased their fire; then the "75's" took
up the tale and plastered the front and communication trenches with shrapnel; then a skir-
mishing line advanced to report the damage done;
and finally the infantry moved forward to an easy

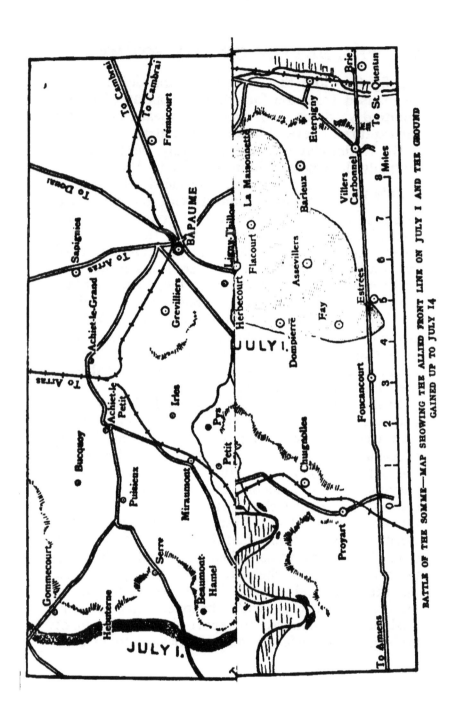

BATTLE OF THE SOMME—MAP SHOWING THE ALLIED FRONT LINE ON JULY 1 AND THE GROUND
GAINED UP TO JULY 14

occupation. It had been the German method at Verdun; but it was practised by the French with far greater precision, and with far better fighting material.

On Monday, 3rd July, they were into the German second position south of the Somme. Twelve German battalions were hurried up from the Aisne, only to be destroyed. By the *July 3.* next day the Foreign Legion in the Colonial Corps had taken Belloy-en-Santerre, a point in the third line. On Wednesday the 35th Corps *July 5.* had the better part of Estrées and were within three miles of Peronne. Counter-attacks by the 17th Division, which had been brought up in support, achieved nothing, and the German railhead was moved from Peronne to Chaulnes. On the night of Sunday, 9th July, Fayolle took Biaches, a mile from Peronne, and the high *July 9.* ground called La Maisonnette, and held a front from there to north of Barleux—a position beyond the German third line. There was now nothing in front of him in this section except the line of the Upper Somme. This was south of the river. North of it he had attained points in the second line, but had not yet carried it wholly from Hem northwards.

The deep and broad wedge which their centre had driven towards Peronne gave the French positions for a flanking fire on the enemy ground on the left. Their artillery, even the heavies, was now far forward in the open, and old peasants beyond the Somme, waiting patiently in their captivity, heard the guns of their countrymen sounding daily nearer. In less than a fortnight Fayolle had, on a front ten miles long, with a maximum depth of six and a half miles, carried 50 square miles of fortifications, and captured 85 guns, vast quantities of war material, 236 officers, and 12,000 men.

The next step was for the British to attack the enemy second position before them. It ran, as we have seen, from Pozières through the Bazentins and *July 13.* Longueval to Guillemont. On Thursday, 13th July, we were in a condition to begin the next stage of our advance. The capture of Contalmaison had been the indispensable preliminary, and immediately following its fall Sir Douglas Haig issued his first summary. "After ten days and nights of continuous fighting, our troops have completed the methodical capture of the whole of the enemy's first system of defence on a front of 14,000 yards. This system of defence consisted of numerous and continuous lines of fire trenches, extending to various depths of from 2,000 to 4,000 yards, and included five strongly fortified villages, numerous heavily wired and entrenched woods, and a large number of immensely strong redoubts. The capture of each of these trenches represented an operation of some importance, and the whole of them are now in our hands." The summary did not err from over-statement. If the northern part of our front, from Thiepval to Gommecourt, had not succeeded, the southern part had steadily bitten its way like a deadly acid into as strong a position as any *terrain* of the campaign could show. The Allies had already attracted against them the bulk of the available German reserves, and had largely destroyed them. The strength of their plan lay in its deliberateness, and the mathematical sequence of its stages.

CHAPTER III

The British Attack on German Second Position—The Fête-Day of
France—The Front attacked—British Dispositions—The Eve of
the Attack—The Wood of Trônes cleared—Capture of Bazentin-le-Petit, Bazentin-le-Grand, and Longueval—High Wood entered—British Cavalry in Action—Fight of the South Africans
in Delville Wood—Fate of the 3rd Guard and 5th Brandenburg
Divisions—Fall of Ovillers—Capture of Waterlot Farm—Difficulty of Longueval Position—British and German Losses—German and Allied *Moral*—The Attack on Pozières—Bad Weather
—First Attack on Guillemont—Capture of Pozières—The Australians in Action—The Fight for the Windmill—Capture of the
Windmill—Failure at Guillemont—Advance toward Mouquet
Farm—German Disorganisation—The Somme Offensive compared
with Verdun—Quality of British Forces—Records of Heroism—
Great French Advance—British carry Leipzig Redoubt—Failure
of Attack on Guillemont—German Counter-attacks—Efficiency of
British Aircraft—French carry Maurepas—Capture of Mouquet
Farm—Fall of Guillemont—Leuze Wood occupied—French 10th
Army comes into Action—French Advance north of the Somme
—Fall of Ginchy—French cut Chaulnes-Roye Railway—End of
First Phase—Capture of German Prepared Positions.

A T dawn on Friday, the 14th, began the second
stage of the battle.
The most methodical action has its gamb-
ling element, its moments when a risk must be
boldly taken. Without such hazards *July* 14.
there can be no chance of surprise.
The British attack of 14th July had much of this
calculated audacity. In certain parts—as at Con-

talmaison Villa and Mametz Wood—we held positions within a few hundred yards of the enemy's line.   But in the section from Bazentin-le-Grand to Longueval there was a long advance—in some places almost a mile—before us up the slopes north of Caterpillar Valley.   On the extreme right the Wood of Trônes gave us a somewhat indifferent place of assembly.   "The decision," wrote Sir Douglas Haig, "to attempt a night attack of this magnitude with an army, the bulk of which had been raised since the beginning of the war, was perhaps the highest tribute that could be paid to the quality of our troops."

The difficulties before the British attack were so great that more than one distinguished French officer doubted its possibility.   One British General, in conversation with a French Colleague, undertook, if the thing did not succeed, to eat his hat.   When about noon on the 14th the French General heard what had happened, he is reported to have observed: "C'est bien! le General X ne mange pas son chapeau!"   It was a pleasant reflection for the British troops that they had surprised their Allies; France had so often during the campaign exceeded the wildest expectations of her friends.

The day of the attack was of fortunate omen, for the 14th of July was the anniversary of the fall of the Bastille, the fête-day of France.   In Paris there was such a parade as that city had not seen in its long history—a procession of Allied troops, Belgians, Russians, British infantry, and last of all, the blue-coated heroes of France's incomparable line.   It was a shining proof to the world of the unity of the Alliance.   And on the same day, while

IN THE TRENCHES NEAR THIEPVAL

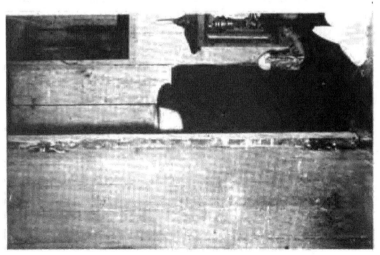

COMFORT IN A DUG-OUT

the Paris crowd was cheering the Scottish pipers as they swung down the boulevards, the British troops in Picardy were breaking through the German line, crying *Vive la France!* in all varieties of accent. It was France's Day in the eyes of every soldier, the sacred day of that people whom in farm and village and trench they had come to reverence and love.

The front chosen for attack was from a point south-east of Pozières to Longueval and Delville Wood, a space of some four miles. Incidentally, it was necessary for our right flank to clear out the Wood of Trônes. Each village in the second line had its adjacent or enfolding wood—Bazentin-le-Petit, Bazentin-le-Grand, and at Longueval the big wood of Delville. In the centre, a mile and more beyond the German position, the wood of Foureaux, which we called High Wood, hung like a dark cloud on the sky line.

The British plan was for the 3rd Corps on the left to form a defensive flank, pushing out patrols in the direction of Pozières. On its right the 15th Corps moved against Bazentin-le-Petit Wood and village, and the slopes leading up to High Wood. On their right, again, the 13th Corps was to take Bazentin-le-Grand, to carry Longueval and Delville Wood, and to clear Trônes Wood and form a defensive flank. In the event of a rapid success the occasion might arise for the use of cavalry, so cavalry divisions were put under the orders of the two corps. The preceding bombardment was to be assisted by the French heavy guns firing on Ginchy, Guillemont, and Leuze and Bouleaux Woods. In order to distract the enemy, the 8th Corps north of the Ancre attacked with gas and smoke as if theirs was to be the main area of our effort.

It was only the day before that we had consolidated our new line, and the work required to prepare for the attack was colossal. The Germans did not believe in an immediate assault, and when the bombardment began they thought it was no more than one of the spasmodic "preparations" with which we had already cloaked our purpose. In the small hours of the morning our guns opened and continued in a crescendo till 3.20 a.m., when the final hurricane fell. An observer* has described the spectacle:—

"It was a thick night, the sky veiled in clouds, mottled and hurrying clouds, through which only one planet shone serene and steadily high up in the eastern sky. But the wonderful and appalling thing was the belt of flame which fringed a great arc of the horizon before us. It was not, of course, a steady flame, but it was one which never went out, rising and falling, flashing and flickering, half dimmed with its own smoke, against which the stabs and jets of fire from the bursting shells flared out intensely white or dully orange. Out of it all, now here, now there, rose like fountains the great balls of star shells and signal lights—theirs or ours—white and crimson and green. The noise of the shells was terrific, and when the guns near us spoke, not only the air but the earth beneath us shook. All the while, too, overhead, amid all the clamour and shock, in the darkness and no less as night paled to day, the larks sang. Only now and again would the song be audible, but whenever there was an interval between the roaring of the nearer guns, above all the distant tumult, it came down clear and very beautiful by contrast. Nor was the lark the only bird that was awake, for close by us, somewhere in the dark, a quail kept constantly urging us—or the guns—to be *Quick-be-quick*."

* The *Times* correspondent.

At 3.25 a.m., when the cloudy dawn had fully come, the infantry attacked. In some places they had had to cover a long distance before reaching their striking-point. So complete was the surprise that, in the dark the battalions which had the farthest road to go came within 200 yards of the enemy's wire with scarcely a casualty. When the German *barrage* came it fell behind them.

The attack failed nowhere. In some parts it was slower than others—where the enemy's defence had been less comprehensively destroyed, but by the afternoon all our tasks had been accomplished. To take one instance. The two attacking brigades of one division were each composed of two battalions of the New Army and two of the old Regulars. The general commanding put the four new battalions into the first line. The experiment proved the worth of the new troops, for a little after midday their work was done, their part of the German second line was taken, and 662 unwounded men, 36 officers (including a battalion commander), 4 howitzers, 4 field guns, and 14 machine guns were in their hands. One division had Bazentin-le-Petit Wood and village, and a second was far up the slopes towards High Wood, after taking Bazentin-le-Grand Wood; another had Bazentin-le-Grand, and another had all but a portion of Longueval. Trônes Wood had been cleared, and a line was held eastward to Maltzhorn Farm. By the evening we had the whole second line from Bazentin-le-Petit to Longueval, a front of over three miles, and in the twenty-four hours' battle we took over 2,000 prisoners, many of them of the 3rd Division of the German Guard. The audacious enterprise had been crowned with a miraculous success.

In the Wood of Trônes on our right flank occurred one of the most romantic incidents of the action. On Thursday night an attack had been delivered there, and 170 men of the Royal West Kents became separated from their battalion. They had machine guns with them and sufficient ammunition, so they were able to fortify one or two posts which they maintained all night against tremendous odds. Next morning the British sweep retrieved them, and the position they had maintained gave our troops invaluable aid in the clearing of the wood. All through this Battle of the Somme there were similar incidents; an advance would go too far and the point would be cut off, but that point would succeed in maintaining itself till a fresh advance reclaimed it. A better proof of discipline and resolution could not be desired.

But the great event of the day fell in the late afternoon. One division, pushing northward against the 10th Bavarian Division, penetrated the enemy's third position at High Wood, having their flank supported by cavalry. It was 6.15 p.m. when the advance was made, the first in eighteen months which had seen the use of mounted men. In the Champagne battle of 25th September the French had used some squadrons of General Baratier's Colonial Horse in the ground between the first and second German lines to sweep up prisoners and capture guns. This tactical expedient was now followed by the British, with the difference that in Champagne the fortified second line had not been taken, while in Picardy we were through the two main fortifications and operating against a more or less improvised position. The cavalry used were a troop of the Dragoon Guards and a troop of Deccan Horse. They made their way up the shallow valley beyond Bazentin-le-Grand, finding cover in the slope of the ground and the growing corn. The final advance, about 8 p.m., was made partly on foot and partly on horseback, and the enemy in the corn were ridden down, captured, or slain with lance and sabre. The cavalry then set to work to entrench themselves, to protect the flank of the advancing infantry in High Wood. It was a clean and workmanlike job, and the news of it exhilarated the whole line. That cavalry should be used at all seemed to forecast the end of the long trench fighting and the beginning of a campaign in the open.

On Saturday, 15th July, we were busy consolidating the ground won, and at some points pushing farther. Our aircraft, in spite of the haze, were never idle, and in twenty-four *July 15.* hours they destroyed four Fokkers, three biplanes, and a double-engined plane, without the loss of a single machine. On the left we fought our way to the skirts of Pozières, attacked the Leipzig Redoubt, south of Thiepval, and continued the struggle for Ovillers. We also advanced against the new switch line with which the Germans connected the uncaptured portion of the second position with their third. We lost most of High Wood under the pressure of counter-attacks by the German 7th Division, and next day we withdrew all troops from the place. They had done their work, and had formed a screen behind which we had consolidated our line.

On the right, around Longueval and Delville

Wood, was being waged the fiercest contest of all. The position there was now an awkward salient, for our front ran on one side westward to Pozières, and on the other southward to Maltzhorn Farm. The division concerned had on the 14th taken the greater part of the village, and on the morning of the 15th its reserve brigade (the South African under Briga-

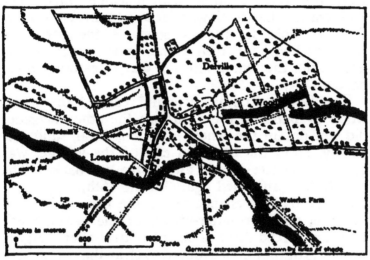

BATTLE OF THE SOMME.—LONGUEVAL AND DELVILLE WOOD.

dier-General Lukin) was ordered to clear the wood. The struggle which began on that Saturday before dawn was to last for thirteen days, and to prove one of the costliest episodes of the whole battle. The situation was an ideal one for the defence. Longueval lies to the south-west of the wood, a straggling village with orchards at its northern end where the road climbs towards Flers. Delville itself was a mass of broken tree trunks, matted undergrowth,

and shell holes. It had rides cut in it, running from
north to south and from east to west, which were
called by such names as "The Strand" and "Princes
Street," and along these were the enemy trenches.
The place was terribly at the mercy of the enemy
guns, and on the north and south-east sides the Germans had a strong trench line, some seventy yards
from the trees, bristling with machine guns. The
problem for the attack was far less to carry the wood
than to hold it, for as soon as the perimeter
was reached, our men came under machine-gun
fire, while the whole interior was incessantly bombarded.

The South African Brigade* carried the whole
wood by noon on the 15th, but the other brigades
did not obtain the whole of Longueval, and the
enemy, from the northern end of the village, was
able to counter-attack and force us back. The
South Africans tried again on the 16th, *July 16.*
but they had no chance under the hos-
tile fire, and a counter-attack of the German 8th
Division forced them in on the central alley. Again
on the 17th they endeavoured to clear the *July 17.*
place, and again with heavy losses they
failed. But they clung desperately to the south-west
corner, and it was not until the 20th that they were
relieved. This is not the place to tell the detailed

---

* The Brigade had already fought in Egypt against the
Senussi. It was composed of the 1st South African Infantry
Battalion (Lieutenant-Colonel Dawson) drawn from the
Cape; the 2nd Battalion (Lieutenant-Colonel Tanner) from
Natal, Orange River Colony, and the Border district; the
3rd Battalion (Lieutenant-Colonel Thackeray) from the
Transvaal; and the 4th Battalion (Lieutenant-Colonel Jones)
from Scotsmen throughout South Africa.

story of those days; but it may be hoped that, for the sake of the British Army and South Africa, the tactical history of that stand will be written. For four days the heroic remnant, under Lieutenant-Colonel Thackeray of the 3rd Battalion, along with the Scots of the other brigades, wrestled in hand-to-hand fighting such as the American armies knew in the last Wilderness Campaign. Their assault had been splendid, but their defence was a greater exploit. They hung on without food or water, while their ranks were terribly thinned, and at the end *July* 20.   when one battalion had lost all its officers, they repulsed an attack by the German 5th Division, the *corps d'élite* of Brandenburg. In this far-flung battle all parts of the empire won fame, and not least was the glory of the South African contingent.*

In this stage of the action we tried conclusions with two of the most celebrated of the German formations. For some days we had engaged the 3rd Guard Division—that division which in April had been brought from the Russian front, and had been hailed by the Kaiser as the hope of his throne and empire. It contained three regiments—the Guards Fusiliers, the Lehr Regiment, and the 9th Grenadiers—and every one had suffered heavily. Some of them showed fine fighting quality, such as the garrison at Ovillers, but they met something more than their match in our New Army. About the 20th of the month the 5th Brandenburg Division appeared, that division which had attacked at Douaumont on 25th February and at Vaux on 9th March.

* Delville Wood was not wholly in our hands till the attack of 25th August.

PIPERS OF THE BLACK WATCH AFTER THE CAPTURE OF LONGUEVAL

A TRENCH AT OVILLERS

Now it was virtually a new formation, for at Verdun it had lost considerably more than its original strength. It was scarcely more fortunate at Longueval. "The enemy," said the Kaiser, in his address on 20th April, "has prepared his own soup, and now he must sup it, and I look to you to see to it. May the appearance of the 3rd Guards Division inform him what soldiers are facing him." The information had been conveyed to us, and our men were by no means depressed. They desired to meet with the best that Germany could produce, for they were confident that they could put that best out of action.

On Sunday, the 16th, Ovillers was at last completely taken after a stout defence, and the way was prepared for a general assault on Pozières. That day, too, on our right we *July* 16. widened the gap in the German front by the capture of Waterlot Farm, half-way between Longueval and Guillemont. The weather broke from the 16th to the 18th, and drenching rain and low mists made progress difficult. The enemy had got up many new batteries, whose positions could not be detected in such weather by our aircraft. He himself was better off, since we were fighting on ground he had once held, and he had the register of our trench lines and most of our possible gun positions. Our situation at Longueval was now an uncomfortable salient, and it was necessary to broaden it by pushing out towards High Wood. On the 20th, accordingly, the 7th Division attacked again at High Wood, and carried all of it except the north part. A trench line ran across that north corner, where the prospect began to open towards Flers and Le Sars. The position was held with extraordinary resolution by the 8th Division of the 4th (Magdeburg) Corps, and it was two months from the first assault before the whole wood was in our possession.

The total of unwounded prisoners in British hands at this stage was 189 officers and 10,779 men. The armament taken included five 8-inch and three 6-inch howitzers, four 6-inch guns, five other heavies, thirty-seven field guns, thirty trench mortars, and sixty-six machine guns. Of the German losses in dead and wounded no exact estimate is possible, but they were beyond doubt very great, and their abortive counter-attacks had probably already brought up the total of the defence to a figure as high as that of the attack. Captured letters all told the same tale. Instant relief was begged for; one battalion consisted of three officers, two N.C.O.'s, and nineteen men; another was so exhausted that it could no longer be employed; another had completely lost its fighting spirit.

No British soldier decried the quality of his opponents. At the most he declared that it was "patchy," which was the truth. There were extraordinarily gallant elements in the German ranks, but they were watered down with much indifferent stuff. Many had lost heart for the fight; they had been told so often of victory assured that they ended by disbelieving everything. On one occasion a hundred men put up their hands while actually charging. Distressful letters from their homes, a lack of confidence in their officers and enthusiasm for their cause, and the suspicion which comes from a foolish censoring of all truth, had impaired the fibre of men who in normal circumstances would have fought stoutly. The German machine was still formidable, but its motive power was weakening.

As for the Allies, every day that passed nerved and steeled them. The French had made the final resolution and the ultimate sacrifice, and of the same quality was the British temper. "Most of these men," said a chaplain, "never handled a gun till they joined up. Yet they have faced bigger things than any veteran ever faced before, and faced them steadily, seeing it all very clearly and fearing it not one scrap; though they have again and again forced mad fear into the highly trained troops facing them. That is because they have something that you cannot make in foundries, that you cannot even give by training. I could give it a name the Church would recognise. Let's say they know their cause is good, as they very surely do. The Germans may write on their badges that God is with them, but our men—they know."

The next step was to round off our capture of the enemy second position, and consolidate our ground, for it was very certain that the Germans would not be content to leave us in quiet possession. The second line being lost from east of Pozières to Delville Wood, the enemy was compelled to make a switch line to connect his third position with an uncaptured point in his second, such as Pozières. Fighting continued in the skirts of Delville, and among the orchards of Longueval, which had to be taken one by one. Apart from this general activity, our two main objectives were Pozières and Guillemont. The first, with the Windmill beyond it, was part of the crest of the

Thiepval plateau. Our aim was the crown of the ridge, the watershed, which would give us direct observation over all the rolling country to the east. The vital points on this watershed were Mouquet

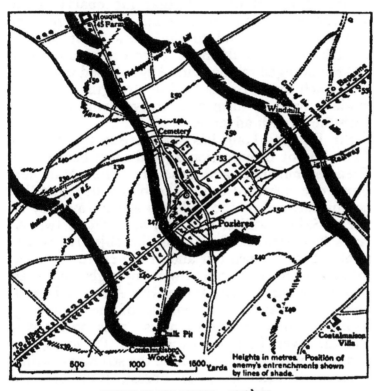

BATTLE OF THE SOMME.—POZIÈRES.

Farm, between Thiepval and Pozières; the Windmill, now only a stone pedestal, on the high road east of Pozières; High Wood; and the high ground direct east of Longueval. Guillemont was necessary to us before we could align our next advance

with that of the French. Its special difficulties lay
in the fact that the approach to it from Trônes Wood
lay over a perfectly bare and open piece of country;
that the enemy had excellent direct observation from
Leuze Wood in its rear; that the quarry on its
western edge had been made into a strong redoubt;
and that the ground to the south of it between
Maltzhorn and Falfemont Farms was broken by
a three-pronged ravine, with Angle Wood in the centre, which the Germans held in strength, and which
made it hard to form a defensive flank or link up
with the French advance.

Sir Douglas Haig has summarised the position:
"The line of demarcation agreed upon between the
French commander and myself ran from Maltzhorn
Farm due eastward to the Combles valley, and then
north-eastward up the valley to a point midway between Sailly-Saillisel and Morval. These two villages had been fixed upon as the objective respectively of the French left and of my right. In order
to advance in co-operation with my right, and eventually to reach Sailly-Saillisel, our Allies had still to
fight their way up that portion of the main ridge
which lies between the Combles valley on the west
and the river Tortille on the east. To do so, they
had to capture in the first place the strongly-fortified
villages of Maurepas, Le Forest, Rancourt, and
Frégicourt, besides many woods and strong systems
of trenches. As the high ground on each side of
the Combles valley commands the slopes of the ridge
on the opposite side, it was essential that the advance
of the two armies should be simultaneous and made
in the closest co-operation."

The weather did not favour us. The third week

of July was rain and fog. The last week and the first fortnight of August saw blazing summer weather, which in that arid and dusty land told severely on men wearing heavy steel helmets and carrying a load of equipment. There was little wind, and a heat-haze lay low on the uplands. This meant poor visibility at a time when air reconnaissance was most vital. Hence the task of counter-bombardment grew very difficult, and the steps in our progress became for the moment slow and irregular. A battle which advances without a hitch exists only in a Staff college *kriegspiel,* and the wise general, in preparing his plans, makes ample allowance for delays.

On 19th July there came the first attempt on Guillemont from Trônes Wood, an attack which *July 19-* failed to advance. On the 20th the *20.* French made fine progress, pushing their front east of Hardecourt beyond the Combles-Cléry light railway, and south of the Somme widening the gap by carrying the whole German defence system from Barleux to Vermandovillers. For the two days following our guns bombarded the whole enemy front, and on the Sunday, 23rd July, came the next great in-*July 23.* fantry attack. Two new corps had been introduced into the Fifth Army from left to right, the 2nd and the 1st Anzac, which took up ground between the Ancre and just south of the Albert-Bapaume road.

That attack had a wide front, but its main fury was on the left, where Pozières and its Windmill crowned the slope up which ran the Albert-Bapaume road. The village had long ere this been pounded flat, the Windmill was a stump, and the trees in the gardens matchwood, but every yard of those devastated acres was fortified in the German fashion with covered trenches, deep dug-outs, and machine-gun emplacements.

The assault was delivered from two sides—a Midland Territorial division moving from the southwest in the ground between Pozières and Ovillers, and an Anzac division from the south-east, advancing from the direction of Contalmaison Villa. The movement began about midnight, and the Midlanders speedily cleared out the defences which the Germans had flung out south of the village to the left of the high road, and held a line along the outskirts of the place in the direction of Thiepval. The Australians had a difficult task—for they had first to take a sunken road parallel with the highway, then a formidable line of trenches, and finally the high road itself which runs straight through the middle of the village.

The Australian troops were second to none in the new British Army. In the famous landing at Gallipoli and in a dozen desperate fights in the peninsula, culminating in the great battle which began on August 6, 1915, they had shown themselves incomparable in the fury of assault and in reckless personal valour. In the grim struggle now beginning they had to face a far heavier fire and far more formidable defences than anything that Gallipoli could show. For their task not gallantry only but perfect discipline and perfect coolness were needed. The splendid troops were equal to the call. They won the high road after desperate fighting in the ruined houses, and established a line where the breath of the road alone separated them from the enemy. A famous division of British regulars on their flank sent them a message to say that they were proud to fight by their side.

When all were gallant it is hard to select special incidents, but in their record of personal bravery the Australians in the West rivalled their famous attack on the Lone Pine position in Gallipoli. The list of Victoria Crosses awarded is sufficient proof. Second-Lieutenant Blackburn led four parties of bombers against a German stronghold and took 250 yards of trench. He then crawled forward with a sergeant to reconnoitre, and, returning, led his men to a capture of a further 120 yards. Private Thomas Cooke, a machine gunner, went on firing when he was the only man left, and was found dead beside his gun. Private William Jackson brought in wounded men from No Man's Land till his arm was blown off by a shell, and then, after obtaining assistance, went out again to find two wounded comrades. Private Martin O'Meara for four days brought in wounded under heavy fire, and carried ammunition to a vital point through an incessant *barrage*. Private John Leak was one of a party which captured a German stronghold. At one moment, when the enemy's bombs were outranging ours, he leaped from the trench, ran forward under close-range machine-gun fire, and bombed the enemy's post. He then jumped into the post and bayoneted three German bombers. Later, when the party was driven back by overwhelming numbers, he was at every stage the last to withdraw. "His courage was amazing," says the official report, "and had such an effect on the enemy that, on the arrival of reinforcements, the whole trench was recaptured."

On Monday and Tuesday the battle continued, and by the evening of the latter day most of Pozières was in our hands. By Wednesday morn- *July 26.* ing, 26th July, the whole village was ours, and the Midlanders on the left were pushing north-ward and had taken two lines of trenches. The two divisions joined hands at the north corner, where they occupied the cemetery, and held a portion of the switch line. Here they lived under a perpetual enemy bombardment. The Germans still held the Windmill, which was the higher ground and gave them a good observation point. The sight of that ridge from the road east of Ovillers was one that no man who saw it was likely to forget. It seemed to be smothered monotonously in smoke and fire. Wafts of the thick heliotrope smell of the lachry-matory shells floated down from it. Out of the dust and glare would come Australian units which had been relieved, long, lean men with the shadows of a great fatigue around their deep-set, far-sighted eyes. They were perfectly cheerful and composed, and no Lowland Scot was ever less inclined to ex-pansive speech. At the most they would admit in their slow, quiet voices that what they had been through had been "some battle."

An observer * with the Australians has described the unceasing bombardment:—

"Hour after hour, day and night, with increasing intensity as the time went on, the enemy rained heavy shell into the area. Now he would send them crashing in on a line south of the road—eight heavy shells at a time, minute after minute,

* Captain C. W. Bean.

followed by a burst of shrapnel. Now he would place a curtain straight across this valley or that till the sky and landscape were blotted out, except for fleeting glimpses seen as
through a lift of fog. . . . Day and night the men worked
through it, fighting the horrid machinery far over the horizon
as if they were fighting Germans hand to hand; building
up whatever it battered down; buried some of them, not once,
but again and again and again. What is a *barrage* against
such troops? They went through it as you would go through
a summer shower, too proud to bend their heads, many of
them, because their mates were looking. I am telling you
of things I have seen. As one of the best of their officers
said to me: 'I have to walk about as if I liked it; what
else can you do when your own men teach you to?'"

Meantime there had been heavy fighting around
Longueval and in Delville Wood. On Thursday,
July 27. the 27th, the wood was cleared all but
its eastern side, and next day the last
enemy outpost in Longueval village was captured.*
July 28. In this action we accounted for the remains of the Brandenburgers, taking
prisoner three officers and 158 men. It was our first
meeting with them since that day on the Aisne, when
they had been forced back by our 1st Division behind
the edge of the plateau. At the same time a Highland Territorial division was almost continuously
engaged at High Wood, where in one week they
made three fruitless attempts to drive the enemy
out of the northern segment. On 23rd July we
attacked Guillemont from the south and west, but
failed, owing to the strength of the enemy's machine-
gun fire.

* The German troops employed in the defence of Longueval
and Delville Wood since 14th July were successively the 6th
Regiment of the 10th Bavarian Division, the 8th Division
of the 4th Corps, and the 5th Division of the 3rd Corps.

Early on the morning of Sunday, the 30th, the Australians attacked at Pozières towards the Windmill, and after a fierce hand-to-hand struggle in the darkness, advanced their front to the edge of the trench labyrinth which con-

July 30.

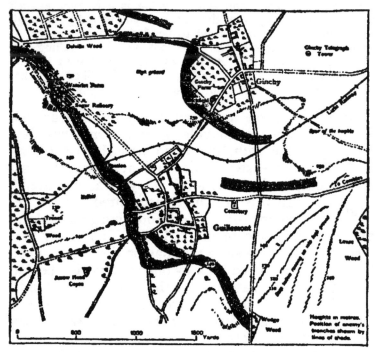

BATTLE OF THE SOMME.—GUILLEMONT AND GINCHY.

stituted that position. Next morning we attacked Guillemont from the north-west and west, while the French pushed almost to the edge of Maurepas. Battalions of the Royal Scots Fusiliers and the Manchesters advanced right through Guillemont, till the

failure of the attack on the left compelled them to
retire, with heavy losses.   Our farthest limit was the
station on the light railway just outside Guillemont
village.

Little happened for some days.   The heat was
now very great, so great that even men inured to
an Australian summer found it hard to bear, and
the maddening haze still muffled the landscape.   We
were aware that the enemy had strengthened his
position, and brought up new troops and batteries.
The French were meantime fighting their way
through the remnants of the German second position north of the Somme between Hem Wood and
Monacu Farm.   There were strong counter-attacks
against Delville Wood, which were beaten off by
our guns before they got to close range.   Daily we
bombarded points in the enemy hinterland, and did
much destruction among their depots and billets
and heavy batteries.   And then on the night of
Aug. 4.   Friday, 4th August, came the final at-
        tack at Pozières.

We had already won the German second position up to the top of the village, where the new
switch line joined on.   The attack was in the nature
of a surprise.   It began at nine in the evening, when
the light was still strong.   An Australian division
advanced on the right at the Windmill, and a New
Army division on the left.   The trenches, which had
been almost obliterated by our guns, were carried
at a rush, and before the darkness came we had
·Aug. 5.   taken the rest of the second position on
        a front of 2,000 yards.   Counter-at-
tacks followed all through the night, but they were
badly co-ordinated, and achieved nothing.   On Sat-

AFTER THE RAIN. AN AMBULANCE STUCK IN THE MUD

urday we had pushed our line north and west of the village from 400 to 600 yards on a front of 3,000. Early on Sunday morning the Germans counter-attacked with liquid fire, and *Aug. 6.* gained a small portion of the trench line, which was speedily recovered. The position was now that we held the much-contested Windmill, and that we extended on the east of the village to the west end of the Switch, while west of Pozières we had pushed so far north that the German line was drooping like the eaves of a steep roof. We had taken some 600 prisoners, and at last we were looking over the watershed.

The following week saw repeated attempts by the enemy to recover his losses. The German bombardment was incessant and intense, and on the high bare scarp around the Windmill our troops had to make heavy drafts on their fortitude. On Tuesday, 8th August, the British right, attacking at 4.20 a.m. in conjunction *Aug. 8.* with the French, closed farther in on Guillemont. At Pozières, too, every day our lines advanced, especially in the angle toward Mouquet Farm, between the village and Thiepval. We were exposed to a flanking fire from Thiepval, and to the exactly ranged heavy batteries around Courcelette and Grandcourt. Our task was to break off and take heavy toll of the many German counter-attacks and on the rebound to win, yard by yard, ground which made our position secure.

In the desperate strain of this fighting there was evidence that the superb German machine was beginning to creak and falter. Hitherto its strength had lain in the automatic precision of its ordering.

Now, since reserves had to be hastily collected from all quarters, there was some fumbling in the direction. Attacks made by half a dozen battalions collected from three divisions, battalions which had never before been brigaded together, were bound to lack the old vigour and cohesion. Units lost direction, Staff work was imperfect, and what should have been a hammer-blow became a loose scrimmage.* A captured letter written by an officer of the German 19th Corps revealed a change from the perfect co-ordination of the first year of war. "The job of relieving yesterday was incredible. From Courcelette we relieved across the open. Our position, of course, was quite different to what we had been told. Our company alone relieved a full battalion, though we were only told to relieve a company of fifty men weakened through casualties. Those we relieved had no idea where the enemy was, how far off he was, or if any of our own troops were in front of us. We got no idea of our supposed position till six o'clock this evening. The English were 400 metres away, the Windmill just over the hill. We shall have to look to it to-night not to get taken prisoners. We have no dug-outs; we dig a hole in the side of a shell hole, and lie and get rheumatism. We get nothing to eat and drink. Yesterday each man drew two bottles of water and three iron rations, and these must last

---

* The German High Command showed themselves good professional soldiers, and did their best to readjust their ideas to meet the new situation. See the report of General Sixt von Armin, which is printed in Appendix II. Von Armin commanded the 4th Corps, and was the general who first entered Brussels in August 1914.

till we are relieved. The ceaseless roar of the guns
is driving us mad, and many of the men are knocked
up." Much of this discomfort was, to be sure, the
fate of any troops in an advanced position, but there
seemed to be an uncertainty as to purpose and a
confusion in Staff work from which the Allies were
now free.

It was the fashion in the German Press, at this
time, to compare the Picardy offensive of the Allies
with the German attack on Verdun, very much to
the advantage of the latter. The deduction was
false. In every military aspect—in the extent of
ground won, in the respective losses, in the accuracy
and weight of artillery, in the quality of the infantry
attacks, and in the precision of the generalship—the
Verdun attack fell far short of the Picardy battle.
The Verdun front, in its operative part, had been
narrower than that of the Somme, but at least ten
more enemy divisions had by the beginning of
August been attracted to Picardy than had appeared
between Avocourt and Vaux up to the end of April.
The Crown Prince at Verdun speedily lost the initiative in any serious sense; on the Somme von
Below and von Gallwitz never possessed it. There
the enemy had to accept battle as the Allied will
imposed it, and no counter-attack could for a moment divert the resolute Allied purpose.*

* The German Commands deserve a note. At the beginning of the battle von Below was in command of the 2nd
Army, but as the attack developed and new troops had to
be brought up, it was found convenient to revive the old
1st Army (abolished since the spring of 1916), and put von
Below in command of it. The 2nd Army farther south was
commanded by von Gallwitz. Later a plan was adopted
similar to the British, and corps commanders were given

We have spoken of the stamina of the British troops, which was never tried more hardly than in the close-quarters fighting in the ruined villages and desolated woods of the German second position. No small part of it was due to the quality of the officers. When our great armies were improvised, the current fear was that a sufficient number of trained officers could not be provided to lead them. But the fear was groundless. The typical public-school boy proved a born leader of men. His good-humour and *camaraderie,* his high sense of duty, his personal gallantry were the qualities most needed in the long months of trench warfare. When the advance came he was equal to the occasion. Much of the fighting was in small units, and the dash and intrepidity of men who a little before had been schoolboys was a notable asset in this struggle of sheer human quality. The younger officers sacrificed themselves freely, and it was the names of platoon commanders that filled most of the casualty lists.

Men fell who promised to win the highest distinction in civilian life. Many died, who were of the stuff from which the future leaders of the British Army would have been drawn. Such, to name one conspicuous instance, was Major William Congreve, who fell at Delville Wood at the age of twenty-five, having in two years of war already proved that he possessed the mind and character of a great soldier.*

groups similar to the British corps, through which a large number of divisions were formed. Among the group commanders were von Stein, von Quast, Sixt von Armin, von Marschall, von Kirchbach, von Hugel, and von Fasbender.

* He was the son of the General commanding the 13th Corps, and had won the D.S.O., the Military Cross, and the

And to take an instance from the French side, on the night of 13th July fell the last Duc de Rohan, who had already been wounded at Verdun in command of his company of Chasseurs. He was killed in the course of a daring night reconnaissance, a young man with great possessions and a great future, who brought to the defence of republican France the proudest blood and most ancient lineage in Europe.* It was a heavy price that the Allies paid, but who shall say that it was not well paid—not only in military results, but in the proof to themselves and to the world that their officers were worthy of their men, and that they realised to the full the pride and duty of leadership?

The list of Victoria Crosses can never be an adequate record of gallantry; it is no more than a sample of what in less conspicuous form was found everywhere in the battle. But in that short list there are exploits of courage and sacrifice which have never been surpassed. Major Loudoun-Shand, of the Yorkshires, fell mortally wounded while leading his men over the parapets, but he insisted on being propped up in a trench and encouraged his battalion till he died. Lieutenant Cather, of the Royal Irish Fusiliers, died while bringing in wounded from No Man's Land and carrying water to those who could not be moved, in full view and under the direct fire of the enemy. Second-

Cross of the Legion of Honour. He received posthumously the Victoria Cross.

* Compare the Rohan motto:
"Roi ne puis.
Prince ne daigne.
Rohan suis."

Lieutenant Simpson Bell, of the Yorkshires, found his company enfiladed, during an attack, by a German machine gun. Of his own initiative he crept with a corporal and a private up a communication trench, crossed the open, and destroyed the machine gun and its gunners, thereby saving many lives and ensuring the success of the British movement. A similar exploit was that of Company Sergeant-Major Carter, of the Royal Sussex, who fell in the attempt. Corporal Sanders, of the West Yorkshires, found himself cut off in the enemy line with a party of thirty men. For two days he held the post, without food or water, and beat off German attacks, till relief came and he brought back his remnant of nineteen to our lines. Private Miller, of the Royal Lancashires, was sent through a heavy *barrage* with a message to which a reply was urgently wanted. Almost at once he was shot through the back, the bullet coming out in front. "In spite of this, with heroic courage and self-sacrifice, he compressed with his hand the gaping wound in his abdomen, delivered his message, staggered back with the answer, and fell at the feet of the officer to whom he delivered it. He gave his life with a supreme devotion to duty." Private Short, of the Yorkshires, was foremost in a bombing attack and refused to go back though severely wounded. Finally his leg was shattered by a shell, but as he lay dying he was adjusting detonators and straightening bomb-pins for his comrades. "For the last eleven months he had always volunteered for dangerous enterprises, and has always set a magnificent example of bravery and devotion to duty."

Officers sacrificed themselves for their men, and

men gave their lives for their officers. Private Veale, of the Devons, went out to look for an officer and found him among standing corn fifty yards from the enemy. He dragged him to a shell hole and went back for water. Then, after vain efforts to bring him in, he went out with a party at dusk, and while they did their work he kept off an enemy patrol with a Lewis gun. Private Turrall, of the Worcesters, when an officer was badly wounded in a bombing attack which had been compelled to fall back, stayed with him for three hours under continuous fire, completely surrounded by the enemy. When a counter-attack made it possible, he carried the officer back to our lines. Private Quigg, of the Royal Irish Rifles, went out seven times under heavy machine-gun and shell fire to look for a lost platoon commander, and for seven hours laboured to bring in wounded. Another type of service was that of Drummer Ritchie, of the Seaforths, who stood on the parapet of an enemy trench sounding the charge to rally men of various units who had lost their leaders and were beginning to retire. And, perhaps the finest of all, there was Private McFadzean, of the Royal Irish Rifles, who, while opening a box of bombs before an attack, let the box slip so that two of the safety-pins fell out. Like Lieutenant Smith, of the East Lancashires, at Gallipoli, he flung himself on the bombs, and the explosion, which blew him to pieces, only injured one other man. "He well knew the danger, being himself a bomber, but without a minute's hesitation he gave his life for his comrades." The General was right who told his hearers that the British soldier had a great soul.

The French by the second week of August had carried all the German third position south of the Somme. On Saturday, 12th August, after preparatory reconnaissances, they attacked the third line north of the river from the east of Hardecourt to opposite Buscourt. It was a superbly organised assault, which on a front of over four miles swept away the enemy trenches and redoubts to an average depth of three-quarters of a mile. They entered the cemetery of Maurepas and the southern slopes of Hill 109 on the Maurepas-Cléry road, and reached the saddle west of Cléry village. By the evening over 1,000 prisoners were in their hands. Four days later, on Wednesday, 16th August, they pushed their left flank —there adjoining the British—north of Maurepas, taking a mile of trenches, and south of that village captured all the enemy line on a front of a mile and a quarter. Except for a few inconsiderable sections the enemy third position opposite the French had gone.

Aug. 12.

Aug. 16.

The British to the north were not yet ready for their grand assault. They had the more difficult ground and the stronger enemy forces against them, and for six weeks had been steadily fighting up hill. At points they had reached the watershed, but they had not won enough of the high ground to give them positions against the German third line on the reverse slopes. The following week was therefore a tale of slow progress to the rim of the plateau, around Pozières, High Wood, and Guillemont. Each day saw something gained by hard fighting. On Sunday, the 13th, it was a section of trench north-west of Pozières, and

Aug. 13-17.

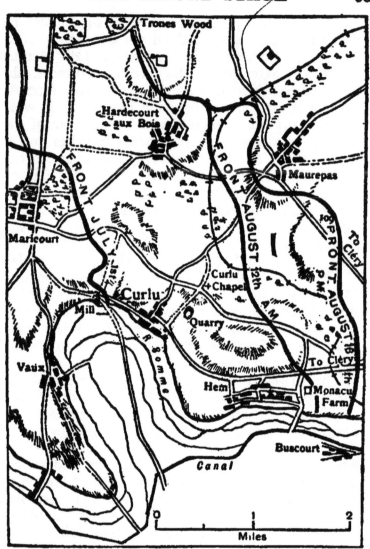

BATTLE OF THE SOMME.—THE FRENCH ADVANCE, AUGUST 12TH–16TH.

another between Bazentin-le-Petit and Martinpuich.
On Tuesday it was ground close to Mouquet Farm.
On Wednesday it was the west and south-west environs of Guillemont and a 300-yards advance at
High Wood.   On Thursday there was progress
north-west of Bazentin-le-Petit towards Martinpuich
and between Ginchy and Guillemont.

On Friday, 18th August, came the next combined
attack.   There was a steady pressure everywhere
Aug. 18.   from Thiepval to the Somme. The main
advance took place at 2.45 in the afternoon, in fantastic weather, with bursts of hot sun-
shine followed by thunderstorms and flights of rain-
bows.   On the left of the front the attack was timed
for 8 a.m.

South of Thiepval, in the old German first line,
was a strong work, the Leipzig Redoubt, into which
we had already bitten.   It was such a stronghold as
we had seen at Beaumont Hamel, a nest of deep
dug-outs and subterranean galleries, well stocked
with machine guns.   As our front moved east to
Pozières and Contalmaison we had neglected this
corner, which had gradually become the apex of a
sharp salient.   It was garrisoned by Prussians of the
29th Regiment, who were confident in the impreg-
nability of their refuge.   They led an easy life, while
their confederates on the crest were crowding in improvised trenches under our shelling.   Those not
on duty slept peacefully in their bunks at night, and
played cards in the deep shelters.   On Friday, after
a sharp and sudden artillery preparation, two British
battalions rushed the redoubt.   We had learned by
this time how to deal with the German machine
guns.   Many of the garrison fought stubbornly to

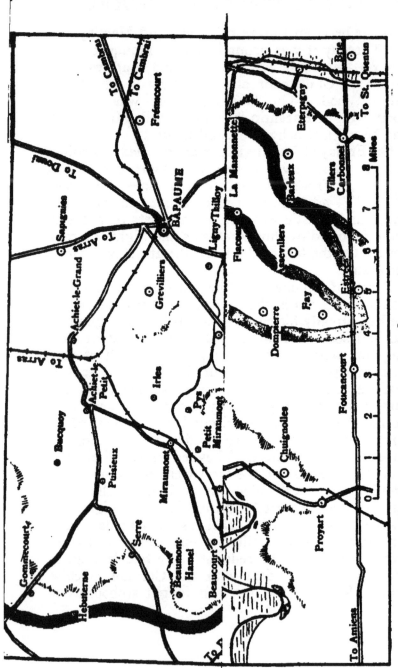

BATTLE OF THE SOMME—ALLIED FRONT ON AUGUST 18 SHOWING THE ORIGINAL LINE ON JULY 1 AND THE GROUND GAINED (SHADED) FROM AUGUST 14 TO AUGUST 18

the end; others we smoked out and rounded up like the occupants of a gambling-house surprised by the police. Six officers and 170 men surrendered in a body. In all, some two thousand Germans were caught in this trap by numbers less than their own. There was no chance of a counter-stroke, for we got our machine guns in position at once, and our artillery caught every enemy attempt in the open.

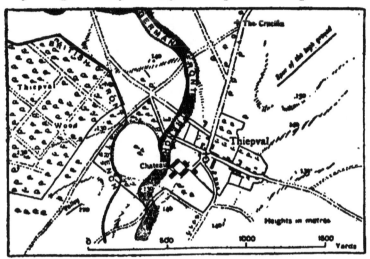

BATTLE OF THE SOMME.—THIEPVAL.

Elsewhere on the front the fighting was harder and less successful. In the centre a famous division pushed closer to Mártinpuich, and from High Wood southward we slightly advanced our lines. We also carried the last orchard in Longueval, and pressed towards the eastern rim of Delville Wood. Farther south we took the stone quarry on the edge of Guillemont after a hand-to-hand struggle of several hours, but failed to hold it. Meantime the

French carried the greater part of Maurepas village, and the place called Calvary Hill to the south-east. This last was a great feat of arms, for they had against them a fresh division of the Prussian Guard (the 2nd), which had seen no serious action for many months.*

We were now fighting on the watershed.   At Thiepval we held the ridge that overlooked the village from the south-east.   We held all the high ground north of Pozières, which gave us a clear view of the country towards Bapaume, and our lines lay 300 yards beyond the Windmill.   We had all the west side of High Wood and the ground between it and the Albert-Bapaume road.   We were half-way between Longueval and Ginchy, and our pincers were encircling Guillemont.   At last we were in position over against, and in direct view of, the German third line.

The next week was occupied in repelling German attempts to recover lost ground, and in efforts to sharpen still further the Thiepval salient and to capture Guillemont.   Thiepval, it should be remembered, was a point in the old German first line on the left flank of the great breach, and Guillemont was the one big position still untaken in the German *Aug. 20.* second line.   On Sunday, the 20th, the Germans shelled our front heavily, and at about noon attacked our new lines on the western side of High Wood.   They reached a portion of our *Aug. 21.* trenches, but were immediately driven out by our infantry.   Next day, at High Wood and at Mouquet Farm, there were frequent

* The whole of the 1st Guard Corps—the 1st and 2nd Divisions—were now facing the French north of the Somme.

THE WORCESTER REGIMENT GOING INTO ACTION

A FIFTEEN-INCH SHELL

bombing attacks which came to nothing. On Tuesday, 22nd August, we advanced steadily on our left, pushing our line to the very edge of what was once Mouquet Farm as well as to the *Aug. 22.* north-east of it, and closing in to within 1,000 yards of Thiepval.

The weather had become clearer, and our counter-battery work silenced some of the enemy's guns, while our aircraft fought many battles. We lost no single machine, but four enemy airplanes were destroyed and many others driven to the ground in a damaged condition. A sentence in a captured letter paid a tribute to the efficiency of the British airmen: "The airmen circle over us and try to do damage, but only enemy ones, for a German airman will not try to come near. Behind the front there is a great crowd of them, but here not one makes his appearance."

Throughout the whole battle there was no question which side possessed the ascendancy in the air. Captured documents bore continual witness to our superiority. One corps report described our air work as "surprisingly bold"; another, emanating from an army headquarters, suggested methods of reorganisation, whereby "it is hoped that it will be possible, at least for some hours, to contest the supremacy in the air of the enemy." Here is the record of the doings of one flight-lieutenant, who encountered a detachment of twelve German machines. "He dived in among them, firing one drum. The formation was broken up. Lieutenant —— then got under the nearest machine and fired one drum at fifteen yards under the pilot's seat, causing the machine to plunge to earth south-east of Baupaume.   Shortly afterwards some more hostile aeroplanes came up in formation.   Lieutenant —— attacked one, which went down and landed in a gap between the woods.   Several other machines were engaged with indecisive results, and, having expended all his ammunition, Lieutenant —— returned."   This was on 1st September, when partridge shooting begins.   Lieutenant —— took the day's work as calmly as if he had been tramping the stubble.

On Wednesday night and Thursday morning a very severe counter-attack on our position at Guille-

Aug. 23-24. mont, pressed with great determination, failed to win any ground.   That afternoon, 24th August, we advanced nearer Thiepval, carrying Hindenburg Trench, and coming, at one point, within 500 yards of the place. In the evening, at five o'clock, the French carried Maurepas, and pushed their right on to the Combles railway, while a light division succeeded at last in clearing Delville Wood.   Next day the French suc-

Aug. 25. cess enabled us to join up with our Allies south-east of Guillemont, where our pincers were now beginning to grip hard.

The following week was one of slow and steady progress.   We cleared the ground immediately north of Delville Wood by a dashing charge of a Rifle Brigade battalion.   The most satisfactory feature of these days was the frequency of the German counter-attacks and their failure.   On

Aug. 26. 26th August, for example, troops of the 4th Division of the Prussian Guard, after a heavy bombardment, attacked south of Thiepval village, and were completely repulsed by the Wiltshire and Worcestershire battalions holding that front. One incident of that day deserves record. A dispatch runner was sent back with a message to the rear, which he reached safely. He started back, came unscathed through the German *barrage,* but in the general ruin of the trench lines failed to find the place he had left. He wandered on and on till he reached something that looked like his old trench, and was just about to enter it when he found it packed with Germans. He immediately jumped to the conclusion that a counter-attack was about to be launched, and, slipping back, managed to reach our own lines, where he told the news. In a minute or two our artillery got on to the spot, and the counter-attack of the Prussian Guard was annihilated before it began. On Thursday evening, 31st August, five violent and futile *Aug.* 31. assaults were made on our front between High Wood and Ginchy, in which a battalion of the Sussex Regiment won great honour. It looked as if the enemy was trying in vain to anticipate the next great stage of our offensive which was now imminent.

On Sunday, 3rd September, at twelve noon, the whole Allied front pressed forward. Australian and British troops attacked on the extreme *Sept.* 3. left—near Mouquet Farm and towards Thiepval, and against the enemy position just north of the Ancre. In their task they encountered the 1st Guard Reserve Division, and took several hundred prisoners. They carried various strong positions, won ground east of Mouquet Farm, and still further narrowed the Thiepval salient. Our centre took High Wood in the afternoon, but pressed on

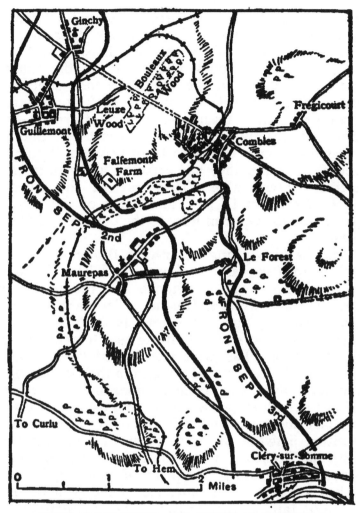

BATTLE OF THE SOMME.—THE ADVANCE OF SEPTEMBER 3.

too far, and had to give ground before a German counter-attack. On their right one division took and lost Ginchy, while another division and one brigade swept through Guillemont to the sunken road, 500 yards to the east. Farther south we attacked but failed to capture Falfemont Farm. Meantime the French—the 1st Corps *—had marched steadily from victory to victory. Shortly after noon, on a 3¾ miles front between Maurepas and the Somme, they had attacked after an intense artillery preparation. They carried the villages of Le Forest and Cléry, and north of the former place won the German lines to the outskirts of Combles.

As the bloody angle south of Beaumont Hamel will be for ever associated with the Ulster Division, so Guillemont was a triumph for the troops of southern and western Ireland. The men of Munster, Leinster, and Connaught broke through the intricate defences of the enemy as a torrent sweeps down rubble. The place was one of the strongest of all the many fortified villages in the German line, and its capture was the most important achievement of the British since the taking of Pozières. It was the last uncaptured point in the old German second position between Mouquet Farm and the junction with the French. It was most resolutely defended, since, being close to the point of junction, it compelled a hiatus in the advance of the Allied front. With its fall the work of two years was swept away,

* The 1st Corps belonged to north-east France, and most of its men came from districts like Lille, Arras, and Roubaix, which had suffered severely from the German occupation. They fought literally to recover their homes.

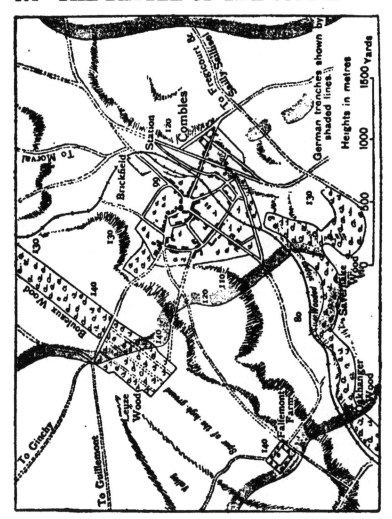

and in the whole section the enemy were now in
new and improvised positions.

But the advance was only beginning. On Monday, 4th September, all enemy counter-attacks were
beaten off, and further ground won by *Sept. 4.*
the British near Falfemont Farm. That
night, in a torrent of rain, our men pressed on, and
before midday on Tuesday, 5th September, they
were nearly a mile east of Guillemont, *Sept. 5.*
and well into Leuze Wood. That even-
ing the whole of the wood was taken, as well as
the hotly disputed Falfemont Farm, and the British
were less than 1,000 yards from the town of Combles, on which the French were pressing in on the .
south.

Meantime, about two in the afternoon, a new
French army came into action south of the Somme
on a front of a dozen miles from Barleux to south
of Chaulnes. This was General Micheler's Tenth
Army, which had been waiting for two months on
the order to advance. At a bound it carried the
whole of the German first position from Vermandovillers to Chilly, a front of nearly three miles,
and took some 3,000 unwounded prisoners. Next
day the French pressed on both north and south
of the river, and in the former area *Sept. 6.*
reached the west end of the Anderlu
Wood, carried the Hôpital Farm, the Rainette Wood,
part of the Marrière Wood, the ridge on which runs
the road from Bouchavesnes to Cléry, and the village
of Omiécourt.

From Wednesday, 6th September, to the night
of Friday, the 8th, the Germans strove in vain to
win back what they had lost. On the whole thirty

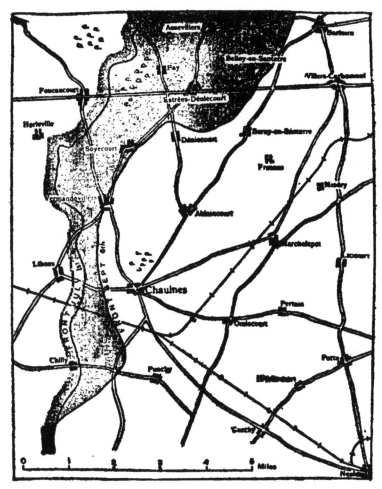

BATTLE OF THE SOMME.—ADVANCE OF MICHELER'S TENTH FRENCH ARMY,
SEPT. 5TH AND 6TH (SHOWING THE ORIGINAL FRENCH FRONT BEFORE
JULY 1ST, AND THE GROUND GAINED BY THE ADVANCE).

THE GROUND GAINED UP TO SEPTEMBER 10TH.
SEPTEMBER 10TH (SHOWING THE ORIGINAL

miles from Thiepval to Chilly there were violent counter-attacks which had no success, though four divisions of the Prussian Guard shared *Sept. 6–8.* in them. The Allied artillery broke up the massed infantry in most cases long before they reached our trenches. On Saturday, 9th September, the same Irish regiments which *Sept. 9.* had helped to take Guillemont carried Ginchy. The attack was delivered at 4.45 in the afternoon, on a broad front, but though highly successful in this one area, it failed elsewhere. We made no progress in High Wood, we were checked east of Delville, and, most important of all, we did not succeed in carrying the work east of Ginchy called the Quadrilateral, which at a later day was to prove a thorn in our side.

Nevertheless the main objects had been attained. The Allied front was now in a symmetrical line, and everywhere on the highest ground. Combles was held in a tight clutch, and the French Tenth Army was within 800 yards of Chaulnes Station, and was holding 2½ miles of the Chaulnes-Roye railway, thereby cutting the chief German line of lateral communication. The first objective which the Allies had set before themselves on 1st July had been amply won.

By the 10th of September the British had made good the old German second position, and had won the crest of the uplands, while the *Sept. 10.* French in their section had advanced almost to the gates of Peronne, and their new army on the right had begun to widen the breach. That moment was in a very real sense the end of a phase, the first and perhaps the most critical phase of the great Western offensive. A man may have saved money so that he can face the beginnings of adversity with cheerfulness; but if the stress continues, his money will come to an end, and he will be no better than his fellows in misfortune. The immense fortifications of her main position represented for Germany the accumulated capital of two years. She had raised these defences when she was stronger than her adversaries in guns and in men. Now she was weaker, and her capital was gone. Thenceforth the campaign entered upon a new stage, new alike in strategical and tactical problems. From Thiepval to Chaulnes the enemy was now in improvised positions. The day of manœuvre battles had not come, but in that section the rigidity of the old trench warfare had vanished.

CHAPTER IV

THE THIRD STAGE

Situation after 3rd September—The German Third Position—The Strain on the Defence—Favourable Outlook for the Allies—Beginning of the New Bombardment—The Allied Plan—The British Dispositions—The "Tanks"—The Battle of 15th September —Fall of Courcelette, Martinpuich, and Flers—High Wood cleared—Check on the British Right—Summary of Results—Achievements of British Aircraft—Death of Raymond Asquith—The French Advance—Capture of the Quadrilateral—The Battle of 25th September—Fall of Morval and Lesbœufs—Battle of 26th September—Fall of Gueudecourt, Combles, and Thiepval—Allied Outlook at Close of September—Nature of the Battleground—The Weather of October—Difficulties of Transport—The Struggle for the Spurs—Its Peculiar Severity—Capture of Regina Trench and the rest of Thiepval Ridge—The French take Sailly—Micheler's Advance—Summary of the Month—Death of Lord Lucas.

THE capture of Guillemont on 3rd September meant the end of the German second position on the whole front between Thiepval and Estrées. The Allies were faced with a new problem, to understand which it is necessary to consider the nature of the defences still before them and the peculiar configuration of the country.

The advance of 1st July had carried the first enemy lines on a broad front, but the failure of the attack between Gommecourt and Thiepval had made the breach eight miles less than the original plan. The advance of 14th July gave us the second

line on a still narrower front—from Bazentin-le-
Petit to Longueval.   The danger now was that the
Allied thrust, if continued, might show a rapidly
narrowing wedge which would result in the formation of a sharp and precarious salient.   Accordingly Sir Douglas Haig broadened the breach by
striking out to left and right, capturing first Pozières
and the high ground at Mouquet Farm, and then—
on his other flank—Guillemont and Ginchy.   These
successes made the gap in the second position some
seven miles wide, and brought the British front in
most places to the highest ground, from which
direct observation was obtainable over the lower
slopes and valley pockets to the east.   We did not
yet hold the complete crown of the ridge, though
at Mouquet Farm and at High Wood we had positions which no superior height commanded.

The German third position had at the beginning
of the battle been only in embryo.   Before the attack of 14th July it had been more or less completed,
and by the beginning of September it had been
greatly elaborated and a fourth position prepared
behind it.   It was based on a string of fortified
villages which lie on the reverse slopes of the main
ridge—Courcelette, Martinpuich, Flers, Lesbœufs,
and Morval.   Behind it was an intermediate line,
with Le Sars, Eaucourt l'Abbaye, and Gueudecourt as strong positions in it; and further back
a fourth position, which lay just west of the Bapaume-Peronne road, covering the villages of Sailly-
Saillisel and Le Transloy.   This was the line protecting Bapaume; the next position, at this moment
only roughly sketched out, lay well to the east of
that town.

Since the battle began the Germans had, up to the second week in September, brought sixty-one divisions into action in the Somme area; seven had been refitted and sent in again; on 14th September they were holding the line with fifteen divisions—which gives us fifty-three as the number which had been used up. The German losses throughout had been high. The French casualties had been singularly light—for they had fought economically under close cover of their guns, and had had, on the whole, the easier tactical problem to face. The British losses had been, beyond doubt, lower than those of the enemy, and our most conspicuous successes, such as the advance of 1st July south of Thiepval and the action of 14th July, had been achieved at a comparatively small cost. Our main casualties arose from the failure north of Thiepval on the first day, and the taking of desperately defended and almost impregnable positions like Delville Wood and Guillemont.

In the ten weeks' battle the enemy had shown many ups and downs of strength. At one moment his whole front would appear to be crumbling; at another the arrival of fresh batteries from Verdun and new troops would solidify his line. The effort had strained his capacity to its full. He had revived the old First Army—which had been in abeyance since the preceding spring—and given it to von Below north of the Somme, while the Second Army, now under von Gallwitz, held the front south of the river. He had placed the Crown Prince of Bavaria, commanding the Sixth Army, in charge of the sector comprising his own and the First and Second Armies. He had followed the British plan of departing from the corps system and creating groups, through which a large number of divisions, drawn from many corps, were successively passed. He had used in his defence the best fighting material he possessed. During those ten weeks almost all the most famous German units had appeared on the Somme—the cream of the Bavarian troops, the Fifth Brandenburgers, and every single division of the Guard and Guard Reserve Corps.

In the early days of September there was evidence that the enemy was in no very happy condition. The loss of Ginchy and Guillemont had enabled the British to come into line with the left wing of Fayolle's great advance, while the fall of certain vital positions on the Thiepval Ridge gave us observation over a great space of country and threatened Thiepval, which was the pivot of all the German defence in the northern section of the battleground. The Allied front north of the Somme had the river as a defensive flank on its right, and might presently have the Ancre to fill the same part on its left. Hence the situation was ripe for a further thrust which, if successful, might give our advance a new orientation. If the German third line could be carried it might be possible to strike out on the flanks, repeating on a far greater scale the practice already followed. Bapaume itself was not the objective, but a thrust north-eastward across the Upper Ancre, which might get behind the great slab of unbroken enemy positions from Thiepval northwards. That would be the ultimate reward of a complete success; in the meantime our task was to break through the enemy's third line and test his powers of resistance.

BRITISH "TANKS" IN ACTION

BRITISH SHELLS BURSTING ON GERMAN TRENCHES

It seemed a propitious moment for a concerted blow. The situation on the whole front was good. Fayolle's left wing had won conspicuous successes and had their spirits high, while Micheler was moving his pincers towards Chaulnes and playing havoc with the main German lateral communications. Elsewhere in Europe things went well for the Allies. On 28th August Rumania had entered the war and her troops were pouring into Transylvania. As it happened, it was a premature and fruitless movement, but it compelled Germany to take instant steps to meet the menace. There had been important changes in the German Higher Commands, and it might reasonably be assumed that von Hindenburg and von Ludendorff were not yet quite at ease in the saddle. Brussilov was still pinning down the Austro-German forces on the Russian front, and Sarrail had just begun his serious offensive in the Balkans. In the event of a real *débâcle* in the West the enemy might be hard pressed to find the men to fill the breach. Every action, it should be remembered, is a packet of surprises. There is an immediate local objective, but on success any one of twenty consequences may follow. The wise commander cannot count on any of these consequences, but he must not neglect them in his calculations. If the gods send him good fortune he must be ready to take it, and he naturally chooses a season when the gods seem propitious.

On Tuesday, 12th September, a comprehensive bombardment began all along the British front from Thiepval to Ginchy. The *Sept.* 12. whole of Sir Henry Rawlinson's Fourth Army was

destined for the action, as well as the right corps—
the First Canadian—of the Fifth Army, while on
the left of the battle to another division was allotted
a preliminary attack, which was partly in the nature
of a feint and partly a necessary preparatory step.
The immediate objective of the different units must
be clearly noted.   On the left of the main front one
Canadian division was directed against Courcelette.
On their right a division of the New Army—that
Scottish division which had won high honour at
Loos—had for its task to clear the remains of the
old Switch line and encircle Martinpuich, but not
—on the first day at any rate—to attempt the capture of what was believed to be a most formidable
stronghold.   Going south, two Territorial divisions
—Northumbrian and London—had to clear High
Wood.   On their right the New Zealanders had
Flers as their objective, while two divisions of the
New Army had to make good the ground east and
north of Delville Wood.   Next to them the Guards
and a division of the old Regulars were to move
north-east from Ginchy against Lesbœufs and Morval, while on the extreme right of the British front
another division of London Territorials were to
carry Bouleaux Wood and form a defensive flank.

It had been agreed between Sir Douglas Haig
and General Foch that Combles should not be directly attacked, but pinched by an advance on both
sides of it.   This advance was no easy problem,
for, in Sir Douglas Haig's words, "the line of the
French advance was narrowed almost to a defile by
the extensive and strongly fortified wood of St.
Pierre Vaast on the one side, and on the other by
the Combles valley."   The closest co-operation was

necessary to enable the two Commands to solve a highly intricate tactical problem.

The British force to be used in the new advance was for the most part fresh. The Guards had not been in action since Loos the previous September, the Canadians were new to the Somme area, while it was the first experience of the New Zealanders on the Western front. Two of the divisions had been some considerable time already in the front trenches, but the others had been brought up for the purpose only a few days before. All the troops were of the best quality, and had a proud record behind them. More perhaps than any other part of the battle this was an action of the British *corps d'élite*.

In this stage, too, a new weapon was to be used. The "tanks," officially known as "Machine Gun Corps, Heavy Section," had come out from home some time before, and had been parked in secluded spots at the back of the front. The world is now familiar with descriptions and pictures of those strange machines, which, shaped like monstrous toads, crawled imperturbably over wire and parapets, butted down houses, shouldered trees aside, and humped themselves over the stoutest walls. They were an experiment which could only be proved in practice, and the design in using them at this stage was principally to find out their weak points, so as to perfect their mechanism for the future. Their main tactical purpose was to clear out redoubts and nests of machine guns which, as we had found to our sorrow at Loos, might hang up the most resolute troops. For this object they must precede the infantry attack, and the task of assembling them before the parapets were crossed was fraught with difficulty, for they were neither silent nor inconspicuous.   The things had been kept a profound secret, and until the very eve of the advance few in the British army had even heard of them.   On 14th September, the day before our attack, some of them were seen by German aeroplanes, and the German troops were warned that the British had some strange new engine.   Rumours also seem to have reached Germany five or six weeks earlier, for orders had been issued to supply the soldiers with a special kind of armour-piercing bullet.   But as to the real nature of the device the Germans had no inkling.

On the night of Thursday, the 14th, the Fifth Army carried out their preliminary task.   On a front *Sept. 14.* of a thousand yards south-east of Thiepval a brigade of the New Army stormed the Hohenzollern trench and the strong redoubt which the Germans called the "Wunderwerk," taking many prisoners and themselves losing little. The fame of this enterprise has been somewhat obscured by the great advance which followed, but it was a most workmanlike and skilful performance, and it had a real effect on the subsequent battle. It deceived the enemy as to the exact terrain of the main assault, and it caused him to launch a counter-attack in an area which was part of the principal battle-ground, with the result that our left wing, after checking his attack, was able to catch him on the rebound.

The morning of Friday, 15th September, was perfect autumn weather, with a light mist filling the hollows and shrouding the slopes.   At 6 a.m.

the British bombardment, which had now lasted for three days, rose to the fury of hurricane *Sept.* 15. fire. The enemy had a thousand guns of all calibres massed against us, and his defences consisted of a triple line of entrenchments and a series of advanced posts manned by machine guns. Our earlier bombardment had cut his wire and destroyed many of his trenches, besides hampering greatly his bringing up of men, rations, and shells. The final twenty minutes of intense fire, slowly creeping forward with our infantry close under its shadow, pinned him to his positions and interfered with his counter-barrage. To an observer it seemed that the deafening crescendo all round the horizon was wholly British.

At twenty minutes past six our men crossed the parapets and moved forward methodically towards the enemy. The Germans, manning their trenches as our guns lengthened, saw through the thin mist inhuman shapes crawling towards them, things like gigantic slugs, spitting fire from their mottled sides. They had been warned of a new weapon, but what mortal weapon was this terror that walked by day? And ere they could collect their dazed wits the British bayonets were upon them.

On the left and centre the attack was instantly successful. The Canadians, after beating off the German counter-attack, carried Courcelette in the afternoon. In this advance French-Canadian troops played a distinguished part in winning back some miles of French soil for their ancient motherland. On their right the Scottish division, which had already been six weeks in line, performed something more than the task allotted it. The capture of

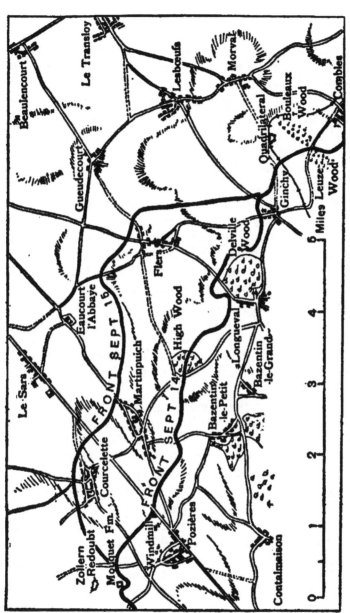

BATTLE OF THE SOMME.—THE BRITISH ATTACK ON SEPTEMBER 15.

Martinpuich was not part of the programme of the day's operations, but the Scots pushed east and west of the village, and at a quarter past five in the evening had the place in their hands. Farther south there was fierce fighting in the old cockpit of High Wood. It was two months since we had first effected an entrance into its ill-omened shades, but we had been forced back, and for long had to be content with its southern corner. The strong German third line—which ran across its northern half on the very crest of the ridge—and the endless craters and machine-gun redoubts made it a desperate nut to crack. We had pushed out horns to east and west of it, but the northern stronghold in the wood itself had defied all our efforts. It was held on that day by troops of the 2nd Bavarian Corps, and the German ranks have shown no better fighting stuff. Our first attack failed, but on a second attempt the London Territorials, a little after noon, swept the place clear, though not without heavy losses.

Beyond them the New Zealand Division, with a New Army Division on its right, carried the Switch line and took Flers with little trouble. They were preceded by a tank, which waddled complacently up the main street of the village, with the enemy's bullets rattling harmlessly off its sides, followed by cheering and laughing British troops. Farther south we advanced our front for nearly a mile and a half. A light division of the New Army, debouching from Delville Wood, cleared Mystery Corner on its eastern side before the general attack began, and then with splendid *élan* pushed forward north of Ginchy in the direction of Lesbœufs.

Only on the right wing was the tale of success incomplete. Ginchy, it will be remembered, had been carried by Irish troops on 9th September, but its environs were not yet fully cleared, and the enemy held the formidable point known as the Quadrilateral. This was situated about 700 yards east of Ginchy at a bend of the Morval road, where it passed through a deep wooded ravine. One of the old Regular divisions was directed against it, with the Guards on their left and the London Territorials on their right. The business of the last-named was to carry Bouleaux Wood and form a defensive flank north of Combles, while the Guards were to advance from Ginchy on Lesbœufs. But the strength of the Quadrilateral foiled the plan. The Londoners did indeed enter Bouleaux Wood, but the division on their left was fatally hung up in front of the Quadrilateral, and this in turn exposed the right flank of the Guards. The Guards Brigades advanced, as they have always advanced, with perfect discipline and courage. But both their flanks were enfiladed; the front of attack was too narrow; the sunken road before them was strongly held by machine guns; they somewhat lost direction; and, in consequence, no part of our right attack gained its full objective. There, and in High Wood, we incurred most of the casualties of the day. The check was the more regrettable since complete success in this area was tactically more important than elsewhere.

But after all deductions were made the day's results were in a high degree satisfactory. We had broken in one day through three of the enemy's main defensive systems, and on a front of over six miles had advanced to an average depth of a mile. It was the most effective blow yet dealt at the enemy by British troops. It gave us not only the high ground between Thiepval and the Combles valley, but placed us well down the forward slopes. "The damage to the enemy's *moral*," said the official summary, "is probably of greater consequence than the seizure of dominating positions and the capture of between four and five thousand prisoners." Three famous Bavarian divisions had been engaged and completely shattered, and the whole enemy front thrown into a state of disorder.

The tanks had, for a new experiment, done wonders. Some of them broke down on the way up, and, of the twenty-four which crossed the German lines, seven came to grief early in the day. The remaining seventeen did brilliant service, some squatting on enemy trenches and clearing them by machine-gun fire, some flattening out uncut wire, others destroying machine-gun nests and redoubts or strong points like the sugar factory at Courcelette. But their moral effect was greater than the material damage they wrought. The sight of those deliberate impersonal engines ruthlessly grinding down the most cherished defences put something like panic into troops who had always prided themselves upon the superior merit of their own fighting "machine." Beyond doubt, too, the presence of the tanks added greatly to the zeal and confidence of our assaulting infantry. An element of sheer comedy was introduced into the grim business of war, and comedy is dear to the heart of the British soldier. The crews of the tanks—which they called His Majesty's Landships—seemed to have acquired some of the light-heartedness of the British sailor. Penned up

in a narrow stuffy space, condemned to a form of
motion compared with which that of the queasiest
vessel was steady, and at the mercy of unknown
perils, these adventurers faced their task with the
zest of a boy on holiday.   With infinite humour
they described how the enemy had surrounded
them when they were stuck, and had tried in vain
to crack their shell, while they themselves sat laughing inside.

In the achievements of the day our aircraft nobly
co-operated.   They destroyed thirteen hostile machines and drove nine more in a broken condition
to ground.   They bombarded enemy headquarters
and vital points on all his railway lines.   They destroyed German kite balloons and so put out the
eyes of the defence.   They guided our artillery fire
and they brought back frequent and accurate reports
of every stage in the infantry advance.   Moreover,
they attacked both enemy artillery and infantry with
their machine-gun fire from a low elevation.   Such
performances were a proof of that resolute and ex-
alted spirit of the offensive which inspired all arms
of the service.   In the week of the action on the
whole Somme battle-ground only fourteen enemy
machines managed to cross our lines, while our airplanes made between two thousand and three
thousand flights far behind the German front.

In the Guards' advance, among many other
gallant and distinguished officers, there fell one
whose death was, in a peculiar sense, a loss to his
country and the future.   Lieutenant Raymond Asquith, of the Grenadier Guards, the eldest son of
the British Prime Minister, died while leading his
men through the fatal enfilading fire from the

HIGHLAND BRIGADE RELIEVED FROM DUTY AFTER THE CAPTURE OF MARTINPUICH

MARTINPUICH MAIN STREET

corner of Ginchy village. In this war the gods took toll of every rank and class. Few generals and statesmen in the Allied nations but had to mourn intimate bereavements, and de Castelnau had given three sons for his country. But the death of Raymond Asquith had a poignancy apart from his birth and position, and it may be permitted to one of his oldest friends to pay his tribute to a heroic memory.

A scholar of the ripe Elizabethan type, a brilliant wit, an accomplished poet, a sound lawyer—these things were borne lightly, for his greatness was not in his attainments but in himself. He had always a curious aloofness towards mere worldly success. He loved the things of the mind for their own sake —good books, good talk, the company of old friends —and the rewards of common ambition seemed to him too trivial for a man's care. He was of the spending type in life, giving freely of the riches of his nature, but asking nothing in return. His carelessness of personal gain, his inability to trim or truckle, and his aloofness from the facile acquaintanceships of the modern world made him incomprehensible to many, and his high fastidiousness gave him a certain air of coldness. Most noble in presence, and with every grace of voice and manner, he moved among men like a being of another race, scornfully detached from the common struggle; and only his friends knew the warmth and loyalty of his soul.

At the outbreak of war he joined a Territorial battalion, from which he was later transferred to the Grenadiers. More than most men he hated the loud bellicosities of politics, and he had never done homage to the deities of the crowd. His critical sense made him chary of enthusiasm, and it was no sudden sentimental fervour that swept him into the Army. He saw his duty, and, though it meant the shattering of every taste and interest, he did it joyfully, and did it to the full. For a little he had a post on the Staff, but applied to be sent back to his battalion, since he wished no privileges. In the Guards he was extraordinarily happy, finding the same kind of light-hearted and high-spirited companionship which had made Oxford for him a place of delectable memories. He was an admirable battalion officer, and thought seriously of taking up the Army as his profession after the war, for he had all the qualities which go to the making of a good soldier.

In our long roll of honour no nobler figure will find a place. He was a type of his country at its best—shy of rhetorical professions, austerely self-respecting, one who hid his devotion under a mask of indifference, and, when the hour came, revealed it only in deeds. Many gave their all for the cause, but few, if any, had so much to give. He loved his youth, and his youth has become eternal. Debonair and brilliant and brave, he is now part of that immortal England which knows not age or weariness or defeat.

Meanwhile the French had not been idle. On Wednesday, 13th September, two days before the British advance, Fayolle carried Bou-

Sept. 13.

chavesnes east of the Bapaume-Peronne road, taking over two thousand prisoners. He was now not three miles from the vital position of Mont St. Quentin—the key of Peronne—facing it across

the little valley of the Tortille. Next day the French
had the farm of Le Priez, south-east of *Sept.* 14.
Combles, and on the afternoon of Sun-
day, the 17th, south of the Somme their right wing
carried the remainder of Vermandovil- *Sept.* 17.
lers and Berny, and the intervening
ground around Deniécourt. The following day
Deniécourt, with its strongly fortified *Sept.* 18.
park, was captured. This gave them
the whole of the Berny-Deniécourt plateau, commanding the lower plateau where stood the villages
of Ablaincourt and Pressoire, and menaced Barleux
—the pivot of enemy resistance south of the river.

For the next week there was a lull in the main
operations while the hammer was swung back for
another blow. On the 16th the 45th Ger- *Sept.* 16.
man Reserve Division counter-attacked
the Canadians at Courcelette, and the 6th Bavarian
Division, newly arrived, struck at the New Zealanders at Flers. Both failed, and south of Combles the
fresh troops of the German 18th Corps succeeded
no better against the French. The most vigorous
counter-strokes were those which the Canadians
received, and which were repeated daily for nearly
a week. Meantime, on Monday, the *Sept.* 18.
18th, the Quadrilateral was carried—
carried by the division which had been blocked by
it three days before. It was not won without a
heavy fight at close quarters, for the garrison resisted stoutly, but we closed in on it from all sides,
and by the evening had pushed our front five hundred yards beyond it to the hollow before Morval.

The week was dull and cloudy, and from the
Monday to the Wednesday it rained without ceas-

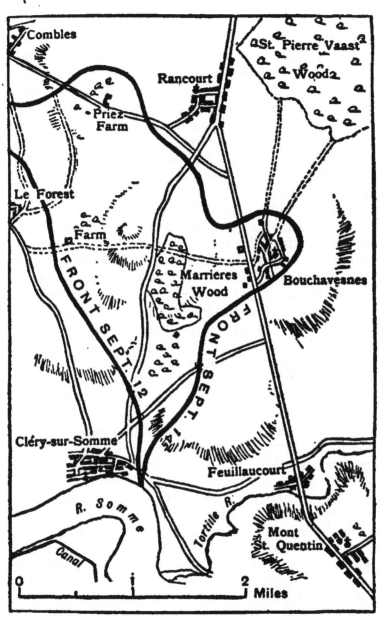

BATTLE OF THE SOMME.—THE FRENCH ADVANCE OF SEPTEMBER 12-14
(CAPTURE OF BOUCHAVESNES AND LE PRIEZ FARM).

ing. But by the Friday it had cleared, though the mornings were now thick with autumn haze, and we were able once more to get that direct observation and aerial reconnaissance which is an indispensable preliminary to a great attack. On Sunday, the 24th, our batteries opened again, this *Sept. 24.* time against the uncaptured points in the German third line like Morval and Lesbœufs, against intermediate positions like Gueudecourt, and especially against Thiepval, which we now commanded from the east. On that day, too, our aircraft destroyed six enemy machines and drove three more to earth. The plan was for an attack by the Fourth Army on Monday, the 25th, with—on its left wing—small local objectives; but, on the right and centre, aiming at completing the captures which had been the ultimate objectives of the advance of the 15th. The following day the right wing of the Fifth Army would come into action, and it was hoped that from Thiepval to Combles the enemy would be driven back to his fourth line of defence and our own front pushed up well within assaulting distance.

The hour of attack on the 25th was fixed at thirty-five minutes after noon. It was bright, cloudless weather, but the heat of the *Sept. 25.* sun had lost its summer strength. That day saw an advance the most perfect yet made in any stage of the battle, for in almost every part of the field we won what we sought. The extreme left of the 3rd Corps was held up north of Courcelette, but the remaining two divisions carried out the tasks assigned to them. So did the centre and left divisions of the 15th Corps, while part

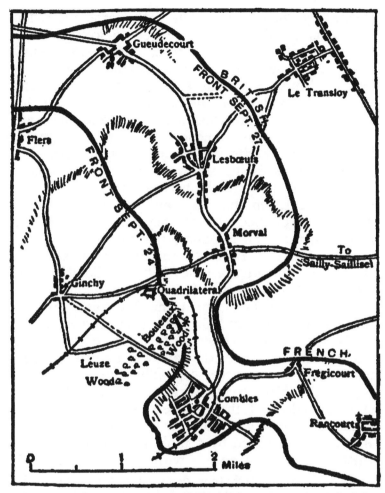

BATTLE OF THE SOMME—THE ATTACK OF SEPTEMBER 25 AND 26 (THE
GAINS ON THE RIGHT).

of the right division managed to penetrate into
Gueudecourt, but was compelled to retire owing
to the supporting brigade on its flank being

checked by uncut wire. The 14th Corps succeeded everywhere. The Guards, eager to avenge their sufferings of the week before, despite the heavy losses on their left, swept irresistibly upon Lesbœufs. South of them a Regular division took Morval—the village on the height north of Combles which, with its subterranean quarries and elaborate trench system, was a most formidable stronghold. The London Territorials on their right formed a defensive flank facing south from Bouleaux Wood. Combles was now fairly between the pincers. It might have fallen that day, but the French attack on Frégicourt failed, though they carried the village of Rancourt on the Bapaume-Peronne road.

By the evening of the 25th the British had stormed an enemy front of six miles between Combles and Martinpuich to a depth of more than a mile. The fall of Morval gave them the last piece of un-captured high ground on that backbone of ridge which runs from Thiepval through High Wood and Ginchy. The next day we reaped in full the fruit of these successes. The divi- *Sept. 26.* sion of the New Army which had entered Gueudecourt the day before—but had failed to maintain their ground, now captured the famous Gird trench, assisted by a tank and an aeroplane—which attacked the enemy with machine-gun fire *

* The official dispatch thus describes this incident: "In the early morning a 'tank' started down the portion of the trench held by the enemy from the north-west, firing its machine guns, and followed by bombers. The enemy could not escape, as we held the trench at its southern end. At the same time an aeroplane flew down the length of the trench, also firing a machine gun at the enemy holding it. These then waved white handkerchiefs in token of surrender, and

—and by the afternoon had the village in their hands. This division was one which had suffered disaster at Loos a year before on that very day, and had, since the beginning of the Somme battle, shown itself resistless in attack. It had already played a large part in the capture of Fricourt; it had cleared Mametz Wood, and it had taken Bazentin-le-Petit Wood on 14th July. It now crowned a brilliant record by the capture of Gueudecourt and an advance to within a mile of the German fourth position. That day, too, the French took Frégicourt, and Combles fell.* The enemy had evacuated it, and, though great stores of material were taken in its catacombs, the number of prisoners was small.

Meantime, on the British left the success was not less conspicuous. Two divisions of the New Army, advancing at twenty-five minutes after noon under the cover of our artillery barrage, had carried Thiepval, the north-west corner of Mouquet Farm, and the Zollern Redoubt on the eastern crest. The German pivot had gone, the pivot which they

when this was reported by the aeroplane the infantry accepted the surrender of the garrison. By 8.30 a.m. the whole trench had been cleared, great numbers of the enemy had been killed, and eight officers and 362 other ranks made prisoners. Our total casualties amounted to five."

* The French 1st Corps entered the line north of the Somme on 23rd August. At the end of six weeks, when they were relieved, they had taken the remainder of Maurepas, and the villages of Le Forest, Bouchavesnes, Rancourt, Frégicourt, and Combles, together with 4,000 prisoners, 23 guns, and 70 machine guns. They believed that they had inflicted at least 40,000 casualties on the enemy. They had the satisfaction of breaking up two divisions of the Prussian Guard, and of advancing two miles on a front of six.

MOVING A BIG GUN

had believed impregnable. So skilful was our barrage that our men were over the German parapets and into the dug-outs before machine guns could be got up to repel them. Here the prisoners were numerous, for the attack was in the nature of a surprise.

On the evening of 26th September the Allied fortunes in the West had never looked brighter. The enemy was now on his fourth line, without the benefit of the high ground, and there was no chance of retrieving his disadvantages by observation from the air. Since 1st July the British alone had taken over twenty-six thousand prisoners, and had engaged thirty-eight German divisions, the flower of the Army, of which twenty-nine had been withdrawn exhausted and broken. The enemy had been compelled to use up his reserves in repeated costly and futile counter-attacks without compelling the Allies to relax for one moment their steady and methodical pressure. Every part of the armies of France and Britain had done gloriously, and the new divisions had shown the courage and discipline of veterans. A hundred captured documents showed that the German *moral* had been shaken and that the German machine was falling badly out of gear. In normal seasons at least another month of fine weather might be reasonably counted on, and in that month further blows might be struck with cumulative force. In France they spoke of a "Picardy summer"—of fair bright days at the end of autumn when the ground was dry and the air of a crystal clearness. A fortnight of such days would suffice for a crowning achievement.

The hope was destined to fail. The guns were

scarcely silent after the great attack of the 26th, when the weather broke, and October was one long succession of tempestuous gales and drenching rains.

To understand the difficulties which untoward weather imposed on the Allied advance, it is necessary to grasp the nature of the fifty square miles of tortured ground which three months' fighting had given them, and over which lay the communications between their firing line and the rear. From a position like the north end of High Wood almost the whole British battle-ground on a clear day was visible to the eye. To reach the place from the old Allied front line some four miles of bad roads had to be traversed. They would have been bad roads in a moorland parish, where they suffered only the transit of the infrequent carrier's cart, for, at the best, they were mere country tracks, casually engineered, and with no solid foundation. But here they had to support such a traffic as the world had scarcely seen before. Not the biggest mining camp or the vastest engineering undertaking had ever produced one tithe of the activity which existed behind each section of the battle line. There were places like Crewe, places like the skirts of Birmingham, places like Aldershot or Salisbury Plain. It has often been pointed out that the immense and complex mechanism of modern armies resembles a series of pyramids which taper to a point as they near the front. Though all modern science had gone to the making of this war, at the end, in spite of every artificial aid, it became elementary, akin in many respects to the days of bows and arrows.

It was true of the whole front, but the Somme

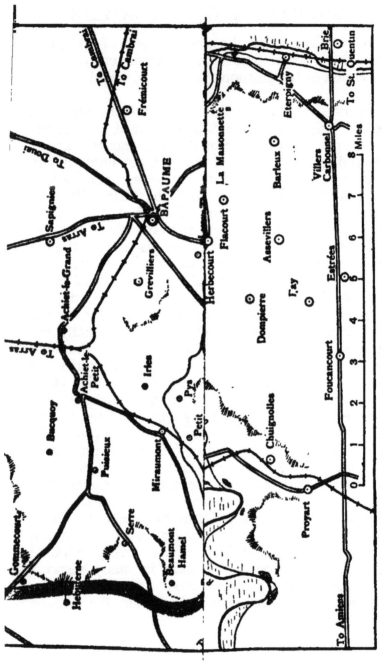

BATTLE OF THE SOMME—THE ALLIED FRONT NORTH OF THE SOMME ON OCTOBER 1ST (SHOWING THE FRONT ON JULY 14TH AND THE GROUND GAINED FROM JULY 14TH TO OCTOBER 1ST)

battle-ground was peculiar in this, that the area of land where the devices of civilisation broke down was far larger than elsewhere. Elsewhere it was defined more or less by the limits of the enemy's observation and fire. On the Somme it was defined by the previous three months' battle. It was not the German guns which made the trouble on the ground between the Albert-Peronne road and the British firing line. Casual bombardments troubled us little. It was the hostile elements and the unkindly nature of Mother Earth.

The country roads had been rutted out of recognition by endless transport, and, since they never had much of a bottom, the toil of the road-menders had nothing to build upon. New roads were hard to make, for the chalky soil was poor and had been so churned up by shelling and the movement of guns and troops that it had lost all cohesion. Countless shells had burst below the ground, causing everywhere subsidences and cavities. There was no stone in the countryside and little wood, so repairing materials had to be brought from a distance, which still further complicated the problem. To mend a road you must give it a rest, but there was little chance of a rest for any of those poor tortured passages. In all the district there were but two good highways, one running at right angles to our front from Albert to Bapaume, the other parallel to our old front line from Albert to Peronne. These, to begin with, were the best type of *routes nationales* —broad, well-engineered, lined with orderly poplars. By the third month of the battle even these were showing signs of wear, and to travel on either in a motor car was a switchback journey. If the famous highroads declined, what was likely to be the condition of the country lanes which rayed around Contalmaison, Longueval, and Guillemont?

Let us take our stand at the northern angle of High Wood. It is only a spectre of a wood, a horrible place of matted tree trunks and crumbling trench lines, full of mementoes of the dead and all the dreadful *débris* of battle. To reach it we have walked across two miles of what once must have been breezy downland, patched with little fields of roots and grain. It is now like a waste brickfield in a decaying suburb, pock-marked with shell-holes, littered with cartridge clips, equipment, fragments of wire, and every kind of tin can. Over all the area hangs the curious, acrid, unwholesome smell of burning, an odour which will always recall to every soldier the immediate front of battle.

The air is clear, and we look from the height over a shallow trough towards the low slopes in front of the Transloy road, behind which lies the German fourth line. Our own front is some thousands of yards off, close under that hillock which is the famous Butte de Warlencourt. Far on our left is the lift of the Thiepval ridge, and nearer us, hidden by the slope, are the ruins of Martinpuich. Le Sars and Eaucourt l'Abbaye are before us, Flers a little to the right, and beyond it Gueudecourt. On our extreme right rise the slopes of Sailly-Saillisel —one can see the shattered trees lining the Bapaume-Peronne road—and, hidden by the fall of the ground, are Lesbœufs and Morval. Behind us are things like scarred patches on the hillsides. They are the remains of the Bazentin woods and the ominous wood of Delville. The whole confines of the British battle-ground lie open to the eye from the Thiepval ridge in the north to the downs which ring the site of Combles.

Look west, and beyond the dreary country we have crossed rise green downs set with woods untouched by shell—the normal, pleasant land of Picardy. Look east, beyond our front line and the smoke puffs, across the Warlencourt and Gueudecourt ridges, and on the sky-line there also appear unbroken woods, and here and there a church spire and the smoke of villages. The German retirement in September had been rapid, and we have reached the fringes of a land as yet little scarred by combat. We are looking at the boundaries of the battlefield. We have pushed the enemy right up to the edge of habitable and undevastated country, but we pay for our success in having behind us a strip of sheer desolation.

There were now two No Man's Lands. One was between the front lines; the other lay between the old enemy front and the front we had won. The second was the bigger problem, for across it must be brought the supplies of a great army. This was a war of motor transport, and we were doing to-day what the Early Victorians pronounced impossible —running the equivalent of steam engines not on prepared tracks, but on highroads, running them day and night in endless relays. And these highroads were not the decent macadamized ways of England, but roads which would be despised in Sutherland or Connaught.

The problem was hard enough in fine weather; but let the rain come and soak the churned-up soil and the whole land became a morass. There was

no *pavé,* as in Flanders, to make a firm causeway.
Every road became a water-course, and in the hollows the mud was as deep as a man's thighs.   An
army must be fed, troops must be relieved, guns
must be supplied, and so there could be no slacken-
ing of the traffic.   Off the roads the ground was a
squelching bog, dug-outs crumbled in, and communication trenches ceased to be.   In areas like Ypres
and Festubert, where the soil was naturally
water-logged, the conditions were worse, but at
Ypres and Festubert we had not six miles of sponge,
varied by mud torrents, across which all transport
must pass.

Weather is a vital condition of success in operations where great armies are concerned, for men and
guns cannot fight on air.   In modern war it is more
urgent than ever, since aerial reconnaissance plays
so great a part, and Napoleon's "fifth element," mud,
grows in importance with the complexity of the fighting machine.   Again, in semi-static trench warfare,
where the same area remains for long the battlefield, the condition of the ground is the first fact
to be reckoned with.   Once we grasp this, the difficulty of the October campaign, waged in almost continuous rain, will be apparent.   But no words can
convey an adequate impression of the Somme area
after a week's downpour.   Its discomforts had to
be endured to be understood.

The topography of the immediate battle-ground
demands a note from the point of view of its tactical
peculiarities.   The British line at the end of September ran from the Schwaben Redoubt, 1,000
yards north of Thiepval, along the ridge to a point
north-east of Courcelette; then just in front of

Martinpuich, Flers, Gueudecourt, and Lesbœufs to
the junction with the French. Morval was now
part of the French area. From Thiepval to the
north-east of Courcelette the line was for the most
part on the crest of the ridge; it then bent southward and followed generally the foot of the eastern
slopes. But a special topographical feature complicated the position. Before our front a shallow
depression ran north-west from north of Sailly-
Saillisel to about 2,000 yards south of Bapaume,
where it turned westward and joined the glen of
the Ancre at Miraumont. From the main Thiepval-
Morval ridge a series of long spurs descended
into this valley, of which two were of special
importance. One was the hammer-headed spur immediately west of Flers, at the western end of which
stood the tumulus called the Butte de Warlencourt.
The other was a spur which, lying across the main
trend of the ground, ran north from Morval to Thilloy, passing 1,000 yards to the east of Gueudecourt.
Behind these spurs lay the German fourth position.
It was in the main a position on reverse slopes, and
so screened from immediate observation, though our
command of the higher ground gave us a view of its
hinterland. Our own possession of the heights, great
though its advantages were, had certain drawbacks,
for it meant that our communications had to make
the descent of the reverse slopes and were thus exposed to some extent to the enemy's observation and
long-range fire.

The next advance of the British army had therefore two distinct objectives. The first—the task of
the Fourth Army—was to carry the two spurs and
so get within assaulting distance of the German

fourth line. Even if the grand assault should be postponed, the possession of the spurs would greatly relieve our situation, by giving us cover for our advanced gun positions and a certain shelter for the bringing up of supplies. It should be remembered that the spurs were not part of the German main front. They were held by the enemy as intermediate positions, and very strongly held—every advantage being taken of sunken roads, buildings, and the undulating nature of the country. They represented for the fourth German line what Contalmaison had represented for the second; till they were carried no general assault on the main front could be undertaken. The second task—that of the Fifth Army—was to master the whole of the high ground on the Thiepval ridge, so as to get direct observation into the Ancre glen and over the uplands north and northeast of it.

The expected fine weather of October did not come. On the contrary, the month provided a record in wet, spells of drenching rain being varied by dull, misty days, so that the sodden land had no chance of drying. The carrying of the spurs—meant as a preliminary step to a general attack—proved an operation so full of difficulties that it occupied all our efforts during the month, and with it all was not completed. The story of these weeks is one of minor operations, local actions with strictly limited objectives undertaken by only a few battalions. In the face of every conceivable difficulty we moved gradually up the intervening slopes.

At first there was a certain briskness in our movement. From Flers north-westward, in front of Eau-

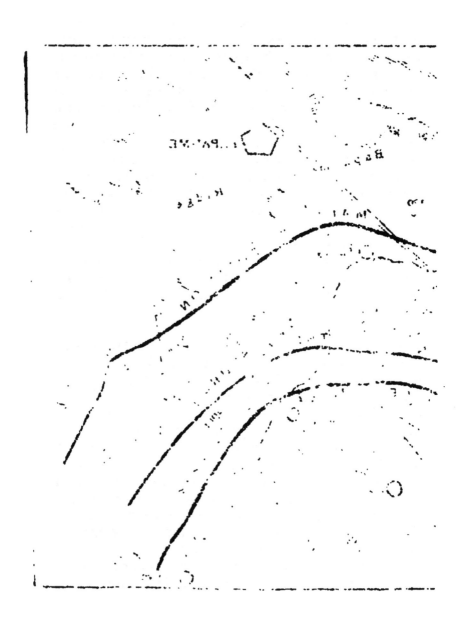

Height in metres

court l'Abbaye and Le Sars, ran a very strong trench system, which we called the Flers line, and which was virtually a switch connecting the old German third line with the intermediate positions in front of the spurs. The capture of Flers gave us the south-eastern part of the line, and the last days of September and the first of October were occupied in winning the remainder of it. On 29th September a single company of a Northumbrian division carried the farm of Destremont, some 400 yards south-west of Le Sars and just north of the Albert-Bapaume road. On the afternoon of 1st October we advanced on a front of 3,000 yards, taking the Flers line north of Destremont, while a London Territorial division—the same which had taken High Wood—occupied the buildings of the old abbey of Eaucourt, less than a mile south-east of Le Sars village. Here for several days remnants of the 6th Bavarian Division made a stout resistance. On the morning of 2nd October the enemy had regained a footing in the abbey, and during the whole of the next day and night the battle fluctuated. It was not till the morning of the 4th that we finally cleared the place, and on 6th October the Londoners won the mill north-west of it.

Sept. 29.

Oct. 1.

Oct. 2.

Oct. 4-6.

On the afternoon of 7th October—a day of cloud and strong winds, but free from rain—we attacked on a broader front, while the French on our right moved against the key position of Sailly-Saillisel. After a heavy struggle a division of the New Army captured Le Sars and won positions to the east and west of it, while our line was

Oct. 7.

considerably advanced between Gueudecourt and Lesbœufs.

From that date for a month on we struggled up the slopes, gaining ground, but never winning the crests. The enemy now followed a new practice. He had his machine guns well back in prepared positions and caught our attack with their long-range fire. To chronicle in detail those indeterminate actions would be a laborious task, and would demand for its elucidation a map on the largest scale. We wrestled for odd lengths of fantastically named trenches which were often three feet deep in water. It was no light job to get out over the slimy parapets, and the bringing up of supplies and the evacuation of the wounded placed a terrible burden on our strength. Under conditions of such grievous discomfort an attack on a comprehensive scale was out of the question, the more when we remember the condition of the area behind our lines. At one moment it seemed as if the Butte had been won. On *Nov. 5.* 5th November we were over it and holding positions on the eastern side, but that night a counter-attack by fresh troops of the 4th Guard Division—who had just come up—forced us to fall back. This was the one successful enemy counter-stroke in this stage of the battle. For the most part they were too weak, if delivered promptly; and when they came later in strength they were broken up by our guns.

The struggle of these days deserves to rank high in the records of British hardihood. The fighting had not the swift pace and the brilliant successes of the September battles. Our men had to fight for minor objectives, and such a task lacks the impetus

and exhilaration of a great combined assault. On many occasions the battle resolved itself into isolated struggles, a handful of men in a mud-hole holding out and consolidating their ground till their post was linked up with our main front. Rain, cold, slow reliefs, the absence of hot food, and sometimes of any food at all, made these episodes a severe test of endurance and devotion. During this period the enemy, amazed at his good fortune, inasmuch as the weather had crippled our advance, fell into a flamboyant mood and represented the result as a triumph of the fighting quality of his own troops. From day to day he announced a series of desperate British assaults invariably repulsed with heavy losses. He spoke of British corps and divisions advancing in massed formation, when, at the most, it had been an affair of a few battalions. Often he announced an attack on a day and in a locality where nothing whatever had happened. It is worth remembering that, except for the highly successful action of 21st October, which we shall presently record, there was no British attack during the month on anything like a large scale, and that the various minor actions, so far from having cost us high, were among the most economical of the campaign.

Our second task, in which we brilliantly succeeded, was to master completely the Thiepval ridge. By the end of September the strong redoubts northeast of the village—called Stuff and Zollern—were in our hands, and on the 28th of that month we had carried all Schwaben Redoubt except the north-west corner. It was Schwaben *Sept.* 28. Redoubt to which the heroic advance of the Ulster

Division had penetrated on the first day of the battle; but next day the advanced posts had been drawn in, and three months had elapsed before we again entered it. It was now a very different place from 1st July. Our guns had pounded it out of recognition; but it remained—from its situation—the pivot of the whole German line on the heights. Thence the trenches called Stuff and Regina ran east for some 5,000 yards to a point north-east of Courcelette. These trenches, representing many of the dominating points of the ridge south of the Ancre, were defended by the enemy with the most admirable tenacity. Between 30th September and 20th October, while we were battling for the last corner of the Schwaben, he delivered not less than eleven counter-attacks against our front in that neighbourhood, counter-attacks which in every case were repulsed with heavy losses. His front was held by the 26th Reserve Division and by Marines of the Naval Division, who had been brought down from the Yser, and who gave a better account of themselves than their previous record had led us to expect. A captured German regimental order, dated

Oct. 20. 20th October, emphasised the necessity of regaining the Schwaben Redoubt. "Men are to be informed by their immediate superiors that this attack is not merely a matter of retaking a trench because it was formerly in German possession, but that the recapture of an extremely important point is involved. If the enemy remains on the ridge he can blow our artillery in the Ancre valley to pieces, and the protection of the infantry will then be destroyed."

From 20th October to 23rd there came a short spell

of fine weather. There was frost at night, a strong easterly wind dried the ground, and the air conditions were perfect for observation. The enemy was quick to take advantage of the change, and early on the morning of Saturday, 21st October, *Oct. 21.* delivered that attack upon the Schwaben Redoubt for which the order quoted above was a preparation.

The attack was made in strength, and at all points but two were repulsed by our fire before reaching our lines. At two points the Germans entered our trenches, but were promptly driven out, leaving many dead in front of our positions, and five officers and seventy-nine other ranks prisoners in our hands.

This counter-stroke came opportunely for us, for it enabled us to catch the enemy on the rebound. We struck shortly after noon, attacking against the whole length of the Regina trench, with troops of the New Army on our left and centre and the Canadians on our right. The attack was completely successful, for the enemy, disorganised by his failure of the morning, was in no condition for prolonged resistance. We attained all our objectives, taking the whole of Stuff and Regina trenches, pushing out advanced posts well to the north and north-east of Schwaben Redoubt, and establishing our position on the crown of the ridge between the Upper Ancre and Courcelette. In the course of the day we took nearly 1,100 prisoners at the expense of less than 1,200 casualties, many of which were extremely slight. The whole course of the battle showed no more workmanlike performance.

There still remained one small section of the ridge where our position was unsatisfactory. This was at the·extreme eastern end of Regina trench, just west of the Bapaume road. Its capture was achieved

Nov. 10. on the night of 10th November, when we carried it on a front of 1,000 yards. This rounded off our gains and allowed us to dominate the upper valley of the Ancre and the uplands beyond it behind the unbroken German first line from Beaumont Hamel to Serre.

Meantime, during the month, the French armies on our right had pressed forward. At the end of September they had penetrated into St. Pierre Vaast Wood, whose labyrinthine depths extended east of Rancourt and south of Saillisel. The British gains of 26th September filled the whole French nation with enthusiasm, and General Joffre and Sir Douglas Haig exchanged the warmest greetings. The immediate object of the forces under Foch was to cooperate with the British advance by taking the height of Sailly-Saillisel, and so to work round Mont St. Quentin, the main defence of Peronne on the north.

Oct. 4. On 4th October they carried the German intermediate line between Morval and St. Pierre Vaast Wood, and on 8th October—in a

Oct. 8. splendid movement—they swept up the Sailly-Saillisel slopes and won the Bapaume-Peronne road to a point 200 yards from its northern entry into the village. On 10th October

Oct. 10. Micheler's Tenth Army was in action on a front of three miles, and carried the western outskirts of Ablaincourt and the greater part of the wood north-west of Chaulnes, taking nearly

Oct. 15. 1,300 prisoners. On the 15th Fayolle pushed east of Bouchavesnes, and on the same day, south of the Somme, Micheler, after beat-

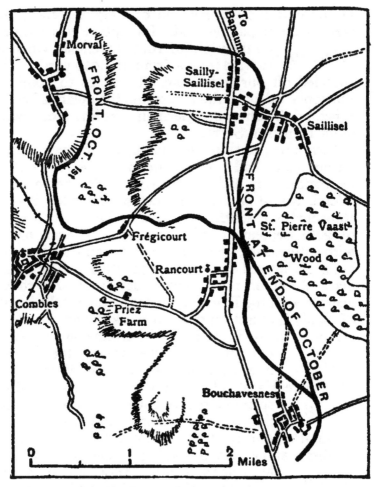

BATTLE OF THE SOMME.—THE FRENCH ADVANCE DURING OCTOBER NORTH
OF THE SOMME.

ing off a counter-attack, carried a mile and a quarter of the German front west of Belloy, and advanced well to the north-east of Ablaincourt, taking some 1,000 prisoners. This brought the French nearer to the ridge of Villers-Carbonnel, behind which the German batteries played the same part for the southern defence of Peronne as Mont St. Quentin did for the northern.

Next day Sailly-Saillisel was entered and occupied as far as the cross-roads, the Saillisel section of *Oct.* 16. the village on the road running eastwards being still in German hands. For the next few days the enemy delivered violent counter-attacks from both north and east, using liquid fire, but they failed to oust the garrison, and that part of the village held by the Germans was mercilessly pounded by the French guns. On the *Oct.* 21. 21st the newly arrived 2nd Bavarian Division made a desperate attack from the southern border of Saillisel and the ridge north-east of St. Pierre Vaast Wood, but failed with many losses. There were other heavy and fruitless counter-strokes south of the Somme in the regions of Biaches and Chaulnes. The month closed with the French holding Sailly but not Saillisel; holding the western skirts of St. Pierre Vaast Wood, and south of the river outflanking Ablaincourt and Chaulnes.

The record of the month, though short of expectations, was far from mediocre; and, considering the difficulties of weather, was not less creditable than that of September. The Allies at one point had broken into the German fourth position, while at others they had won positions of assault against it,

POINTING A HEAVY GUN

HEAVY GUN IN ACTION

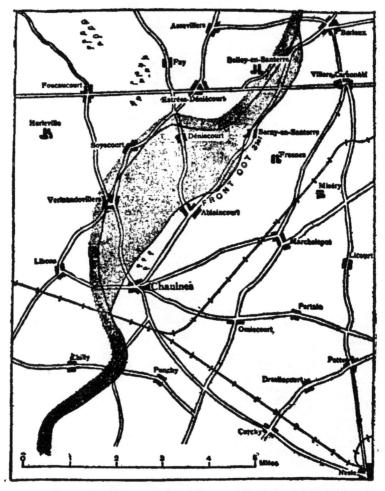

BATTLE OF THE SOMME.—THE FRENCH ADVANCE DURING OCTOBER SOUTH
OF THE SOMME (SHOWING THE FRONT OF THE TENTH ARMY ON OCT.
1ST, AND THE GROUND GAINED DURING THE MONTH).

and the southward extension of the battle-ground had been greatly deepened. They had added another 10,000 prisoners to their roll, bringing the total from 1st July to 1,469 officers and 71,532 other ranks, while they had also taken 173 field guns, 130 heavy pieces, 215 trench mortars, and 988 machine guns. They had engaged ninety enemy divisions, of which twenty-six had been taken out, refitted, and sent back again—making a total of 116 brought into action. On 1st November the enemy was holding his front with twenty-

Nov. 1.

one divisions, so that ninety-five had been used up and withdrawn. Any calculation of enemy losses during the actual progress of operations must be a very rough estimate, but it may be taken for granted that no German division was taken out of the line till it had lost at least 5,000 men. This gives a minimum figure for enemy losses during the four months' battle of close on half a million, and it seems certain that the real figure was at least 25 per cent. greater. It must further be noted that, according to the German published returns, 41 per cent. of their casualties were irreplaceable—dead, prisoners, or so badly wounded as to be useless for the remainder of the war—a proportion greatly in excess of that which obtained among the Allies. During the month of October the British casualties were little beyond those of a normal month of trench warfare.

The study of captured documents cast an interesting light upon the condition of the enemy under the pressure of our attacks. Letters of individual soldiers and the reports of commanding officers alike showed that the strain had been very great. There were constant appeals to troops to hold some point as vital to the whole position, and these points invariably fell into our hands. There were endless complaints of the ruin wrought by our artillery and of the ceaseless activity of our aircraft, and there were many unwilling tributes to the fighting quality of the Allied soldiers. But though indications of weakened enemy *moral* and failure in enemy organisation were frequent, he was still a most formidable antagonist. He had accumulated his best troops and batteries on the Somme front, and was fighting with the stubborn resolution of those who knew that they were facing the final peril, and that they alone stood between their country and defeat.

In the various actions the work of the Allied artillery was extraordinarily efficient. Their barrages brilliantly covered the advance of the infantry; they searched out and silenced enemy batteries; they destroyed great lengths of enemy trenches and countless enemy strongholds; and they kept up a continuous fire behind the enemy's front, interfering with the movement of troops and supplies, and giving him no peace for eight or ten miles behind his line. The "tanks," though only occasionally used, had some remarkable achievements to their credit. On a certain day one got behind the enemy's front, and by itself compelled the surrender of a whole battalion, including the battalion commander. Much credit was due also to the transport service, which faithfully performed its duties under the most trying conditions.

The weather was bad for all, but perhaps it was worst for our aircraft. The strong south-westerly gales greatly increased the complexity of their task, since our machines were drifted far behind the

enemy's front and compelled to return against a
head-wind, which made their progress slow and
thereby exposed them to fire, and, in the case of a
damaged engine, forbade a glide into safety. Yet,
in spite of adverse conditions, they showed in the
highest degree the spirit of the offensive. They
patrolled regularly far behind the enemy lines, and
fought many battles in the air with hostile machines,
and many with enemy troops on the ground. They
did much valuable reconnaissance, and repeatedly
attacked with success enemy lines of communication,
ammunition dumps, billets, and depots. Toward the
latter part of October the German machines were
more in evidence, but we dealt satisfactorily with this
increased activity. As an instance of the audacity
of our aviators we may quote the case of one pilot
who, encountering a formation of ten hostile machines, attacked them single-handed and dispersed
them far behind their own front.

We inflicted many losses on the foe, but we did
not go scathless ourselves. The curt announcement
in the *communiqués*—"One of our machines has not
returned"—covered many a tale of bravery and
misfortune. About half the missing came down in
enemy territory and were made prisoners; the others
perished in battle in the air, shot by machine
or anti-aircraft gun, or dashed to earth by a crippled
airplane. In a flight over the German lines on 4th
November there died one of the most
Nov. 4. gallant figures of our day, conspicuous
even in the universal heroism of his service. Lord
Lucas, whom Oxford of twenty years ago knew as
"Bron Herbert," had joined the Flying Corps at
the age of forty. He had lost a leg in the South

African War; he had had a distinguished political career, culminating in a seat in the Cabinet as President of the Board of Agriculture; he had great possessions and a thousand ties to ease; if ever man might have found his reasonable duty in a less perilous sphere it was he. But after the formation of the Coalition Government in May 1915, he went straight into training for his pilot's certificate, and soon proved himself an exceptionally bold and skilful aviator. He did good work in Egypt, whence he returned in the spring of 1916, and after a few months spent in instructing recruits at home he came out to France in the early autumn. He was one who retained in all his many activities the adventurous zest and the strange endearing simplicity of a boy. With his genius for happiness the world in which he dwelt could never be a common place. In the air he found the pure exultant joy of living that he had always sought, and he passed out of life like some hero of romance, with his ardour undimmed and his dream untarnished.*

* "When the Greeks made their fine saying that those whom the gods love die young, I cannot help believing they had this sort of death in their eye. For surely, at whatever age it overtakes the man, this is to die young. Death has not been suffered to take so much as an illusion from his heart. In the hot-fit of life, a-tiptoe on the highest point of being, he passes at a bound on to the other side. The noise of the mallet and chisel is scarcely quenched, the trumpets are hardly done blowing, when, trailing with him clouds of glory, this happy-starred, full-blooded spirit shoots into the spiritual land."—R. L. STEVENSON. *Æs Triplex*.

CHAPTER V

THE FOURTH STAGE

Improvement in the Weather—The Position North of Thiepval—The British Advantages—British Dispositions—The Battle of the Ancre—Failure at Serre—Ground gained North of Beaumont Hamel—Capture of St. Pierre Divion—The Taking of Beaumont Hamel—Fall of Beaucourt—Lieutenant-Colonel Freyberg's Exploit—Number of Prisoners—Position at End of November—General Results of the Battle of the Somme—The Allied Purposes effected—Sir Douglas Haig's Summary—New German Efforts—Effect of the Battle on German Opinion—The Major Purpose—The British Achievement and its Cost.

O N 9th November the weather improved. The wind swung round to the north and the rain ceased, but owing to the season of the year the ground was slow to dry, and in the area of the
Nov. 9. Fourth Army the roads were still past praying for. Presently frost came and a powder of snow, and then once more the rain. But in the few days of comparatively good conditions the British Commander-in-Chief brought the battle to a fourth stage, and won a conspicuous victory.

On the first day of July, as we have seen, our attack failed on the eight miles between Gommecourt and Thiepval. For four months we drove far into the heart of the German defences farther south, but the stubborn enemy front before Beaumont

Hamel and Serre remained untried. The position was immensely strong, and its holders—not without reason—believed it to be impregnable. All the slopes were tunnelled deep with old catacombs— many of them made originally as hiding-places in the French Wars of Religion—and these had been linked up by passages to constitute a subterranean city, where whole battalions could be assembled. There were endless redoubts and strong points armed with machine guns, as we knew to our cost in July, and the wire entanglements were on a scale which has probably never been paralleled. Looked at from our first line they resembled a solid wall of red rust. Very strong, too, were the sides of the Ancre, should we seek to force a passage that way, and the hamlets of Beaucourt and St. Pierre Divion, one on each bank, were fortresses of the Beaumont Hamel stamp. From Gommecourt to the Thiepval ridge the enemy positions were the old first line ones, prepared dur- ing two years of leisure, and not the improvised de- fences on which they had been thrown back between Thiepval and Chaulnes.

At the beginning of November the area of the Allied pressure was over thirty miles, but we had never lost sight of the necessity of widening the breach. It was desirable, with a view to the winter warfare, that the enemy should be driven out of his prepared defences on the broadest front possible. The scheme of an assault upon the Serre-Ancre line might seem a desperate one so late in the season, but we had learned much since 1st July, and, as compared with that date, we had now certain real advantages. In the first place our whole tactical use of artillery had undergone a change. Our creeping

barrage, moving in front of advancing infantry, protected them to a great extent from the machine-gun
fusilade from parapets and shell holes which had
been our undoing in the earlier battle, and assisted
them in keeping direction.   In the second place our
possession of the whole Thiepval ridge seriously out-
flanked the German front north of the Ancre.   In
the dips of the high ground behind Serre and Beaumont Hamel their batteries had been skilfully em-
placed in the beginning of July, and they had been
able to devote their whole energy to the attack coming from the west.   But now they were facing southward and operating against our lines on the Thiepval
ridge, and we commanded them to some extent by
possessing the higher ground and the better observation.   If, therefore, we should attack again from the
west, supported also by our artillery fire from the
south, the enemy guns would be fighting on two
fronts.   The German position in July had been a
straight line; it was now a salient.

We had two other assets for a November assault.
The slow progress of the Fourth Army during October had led the enemy to conclude that our offensive had ceased for the winter.   Drawing a natural
deduction from the condition of the country, he
·argued that an attack on a grand scale was physically
impossible, especially an attack upon a fortress which
had defied our efforts when we advanced with fresh
troops and unwearied impetus in the height of summer.   Again, the area from Thiepval northward did
not suffer from transport difficulties in the same degree as the southern terrain.   Since we would be
advancing from what was virtually our old front line,
we would escape the problem of crossing five or six

miles of shell-torn ground by roads ploughed up and broken from four months' traffic.

It is necessary to grasp the topographical features of the new battle-ground. From north of the Schwaben Redoubt our front curved sharply to the north-west, crossing the Ancre 500 yards south of the hamlet of St. Pierre Divion, and extending north-ward along the foot of the slopes on which lay the villages of Beaumont Hamel and Serre. From the high ground north-west of the Ancre several clearly marked spurs descend to the upper valley of that stream. The chief is a long ridge with Serre at its western extremity, the village of Puisieux on the north, Beaucourt-sur-Ancre on the south, and Miraumont at the eastern end. South of this there is another feature running from a point a thousand yards north of Beaumont Hamel to the village of Beaucourt. This latter spur has on its south-west side a shallow depression up which runs the Beaucourt-Beaumont Hamel road, and it is defined on the north-east by the Beaucourt-Serre road. All the right bank of the Ancre is thus a country of slopes and pockets. On the left bank there is a stretch of flattish ground under the Thiepval ridge extending up the valley past St. Pierre Divion to Grandcourt.

On Sunday, 12th November, Sir Hubert Gough's Fifth Army held the area from Gommecourt in the north to the Albert-Bapaume road. Op- *Nov.* 12. posite Serre and extending south to a point just north of Beaumont Hamel lay two divisions of the old Regulars, now much changed in composition, but containing battalions that had been through the whole campaign since Mons. In front

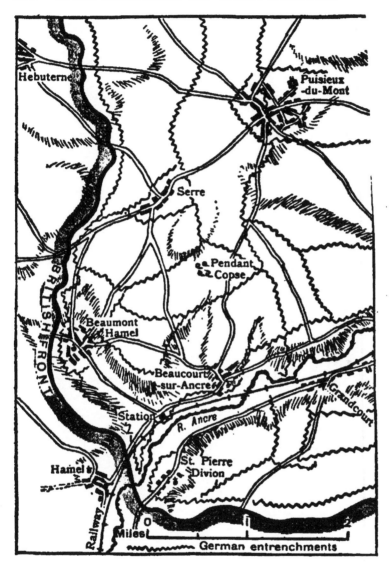

BATTLE OF THE SOMME.—THE BRITISH LINE NORTH OF THIEPVAL ON
NOVEMBER 13.

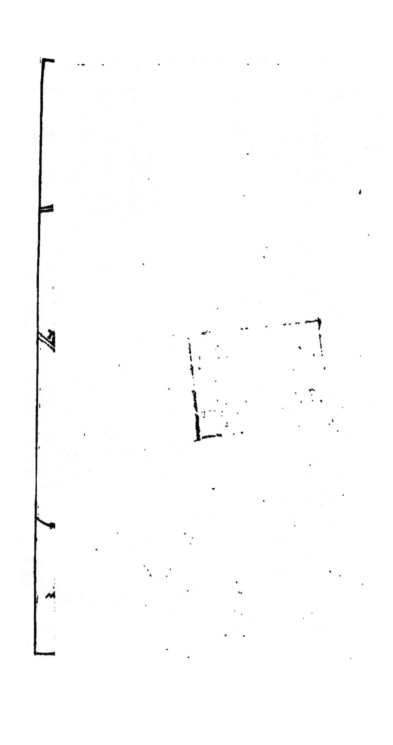

of Beaumont Hamel was a Highland Territorial Division. They had been more than eighteen months in France, and at the end of July and the beginning of August had spent seventeen days in the line at High Wood. On their right, from a point just south of the famous **Y** Ravine to the Ancre, lay the Naval Division, which had had a long record of fighting from Antwerp to Gallipoli, but now for the first time took part in an action on the Western front. Across the river lay two divisions of the New Army. The boundary of the attack on the right was roughly defined by the Thiepval-Grandcourt road.

The British guns began on the morning of Saturday, the 11th, a bombardment devoted to the destruction of the enemy's wire and parapets. It went on fiercely during Sunday, but did not increase to hurricane fire, so that the enemy had no warning of the hour of our attack. In the darkness of the early morning of Monday, 13th November, the fog gathered thick—a cold, raw vapour which wrapped the ground like a garment. It *Nov.* 13. was still black darkness, darker even than the usual moonless winter night, when, at 5.45 a.m., our troops crossed the parapets. The attack had been most carefully planned, but in that dense shroud it was hard for the best trained soldiers to keep direction. On the other hand, the enemy had no warning of our coming till our men were surging over his trenches.

The attack of the British left wing on Serre failed, as it had failed on 1st July. That stronghold, being farther removed from the effect of our flanking fire from the Thiepval ridge, presented all the difficulties which had baffled us at the first attempt. South of it and north of Beaumont Hamel we carried the German first position and swept beyond the fortress called the Quadrilateral—which had proved too hard a knot to unravel four months earlier. This gave us the northern part of the under feature which we have already described as running south-east to Beaucourt. Out right wing had a triumphant progress. Almost at once it gained its objectives. St. Pierre Divion fell early in the morning, and the division of the New Army engaged there advanced a mile and took nearly 1,400 prisoners at a total cost of less than 600 casualties.* By the evening they were holding the Hansa line which runs from the neighbourhood of Stuff trench on the heights to the bank of the river opposite Beaucourt.

But it was on the doings of the two central divisions that the fortune of the day depended, and their achievement was so remarkable and presented so many curious features that it is worth telling in some detail. The Highland Territorials—a kilted division except for their lowland Pioneer battalion—had one of the hardest tasks that had faced troops in the whole battle, a task comparable to the taking of Contalmaison and Guillemont and Delville Wood. They had before them the fortress-village of Beaumont Hamel itself. South of it lay the strong Ridge Redoubt, and south again the Y Ravine, whose prongs projected down to the German front line and whose tail ran back towards Station Road south of the

---

* At one moment the number of prisoners was actually greater than the attacking force.

RUINS OF BEAUMONT HAMEL.

THE RAILWAY AT BEAUCOURT

Cemetery. This **Y** Ravine was some 800 yards long, and in places 30 feet deep, with over-hanging sides. In its precipitous banks were the entrances to the German dug-outs, completely screened from shell fire and connecting farther back by means of tunnels with the great catacombs. Such a position allowed reinforcements to be sent up underground, even though we might be holding all the sides. The four successive German lines were so skilfully linked up subterraneously that they formed virtually a single line, no part of which could be considered to be captured till the whole was taken.

The first assault took the Scots through the German defences on all their front, except just before the ends of the **Y** Ravine. They advanced on both sides of that gully and carried the third enemy line shortly after daybreak. There was much stern fighting in the honeycombed land, but early in the forenoon they had pushed right through the German main position and were pressing beyond Station Road and the hollow where the village lies towards Munich trench and their ultimate objective—the Beaucourt-Serre road. The chief fighting of the day centred round **Y** Ravine. So soon as we had gained the third line on both sides of it our men leaped down the steep sides into the gully. Then followed a desperate struggle, for the entrances to the dug-outs had been obscured by our bombardment, and no man knew from what direction the enemy might appear. About mid-day the eastern part of the ravine was full of our men, but the Germans were in the prongs. Early in the afternoon we delivered a fresh attack from the west and gradually forced the defence to surrender. After

that it became a battle of *nettoyeurs,* small parties
digging out Germans from underground lairs—for
the very strength of his fortifications proved a trap
to the enemy once they had been breached.   If he
failed to prevent our entrance he himself was wholly
unable to get out.

The foggy autumn day was full of wild adven-
tures.   One Scots officer and two men, who took
prisoner a German battalion commander and his
staff, found themselves cut off and the position re-
versed, and then, as supports came up, once more
claimed their captives.   A wounded signaller held up
a German company in a burrow while he telephoned
back for help.   Ration stores were captured and
muddy Highlanders went about the business of war
eating tinned meats with one hand and smoking large
cigars.   By the evening the whole of Beaumont
Hamel was occupied and posts were out as far as
Munich trench, while over 1,400 prisoners and between fifty and sixty machine guns were the prize of
the conquerors.   To their eternal honour the Highland Territorials had stormed, by sheer hand-to-hand
fighting, one of the strongest German forts on the
Western front.

On their right the Naval Division advanced against
Beaucourt, attacking over the ground which had been
partly covered by the left of the Ulster Division on
1st July.   On that day the British trenches had been
between 500 and 700 yards from the German front
line, leaving too great an extent of No Man's Land
to be covered by the attacking infantry.   But before
the present action the Naval Division had dug advanced trenches, and now possessed a line of depart-
ure not more than 250 yards from the enemy.

Their first objective was the German support line,
the second Station Road—which ran from Beaumont
Hamel to the main Albert-Lille railway—and their
third the trench line outside Beaucourt village. The
wave of assault carried our men over the first two
German lines, and for a moment it looked as if the
advance was about to go smoothly forward to its
goal. But in the centre of our front of attack, in a
communication trench between the second and third
German lines and about 800 yards from the river
bank, was a very strong redoubt manned by machine
guns. This had not been touched by our artillery,
and it effectively blocked the centre of our advance,
while at the same time flanking fire from the slopes
behind Beaumont Hamel checked our left. Various
parties got through and reached the German support line and even as far as Station Road. But at
about 8.30 the situation, as reviewed by the divisional commander, bore an ominous likeness to what
had happened to the Ulstermen on 1st July. Isolated
detachments had gone forward, but the enemy
had manned his reserve trenches behind them,
and the formidable redoubt was blocking any general progress.

At this moment there came news by a pigeon message of the right battalion. It was commanded by
a young New Zealander, Lieutenant-Colonel Freyberg, who had done brilliant service in Gallipoli, and
had before the war been engaged in many adventurous pursuits. The message announced that
his battalion had gone clean through to the third
objective, and was now waiting outside Beaucourt
village for our barrage to lift in order to take the
place. He had led his men along the edge of the

river to Station Road, where he had collected odd parties of other battalions, and at 8.21 had reached Beaucourt trench—a mile distant from our front of assault. On receipt of this startling news a Territorial battalion was sent up to his support, and all that day a precarious avenue of communication for food and ammunition was kept open along the edge of the stream, under such shelter as the banks afforded. A second attack on the whole front was delivered in the afternoon by the supporting brigade of the Naval Division, but this, too, was held up by the redoubt, though again a certain number got through and reached Station Road and even the slopes beyond it. It was at this time that seventeen men of the Dublin Fusiliers, accompanied by a priest, performed a singular feat. Far up on the high ground east of Beaumont Hamel they came upon a large party of Germans in dug-outs, and compelled their surrender. They marched their 400 prisoners stolidly back to our line through the enemy barrage and our own.

That night it was resolved to make a great effort to put the redoubt out of action. Two tanks were brought up, one of which succeeded in getting within range, and the garrison of the stronghold hoisted the white flag. The way was now clear for a general advance next morning, to assist in which a brigade of another division was brought up in sup-

Nov. 14. port. Part of the advance lost direction, but the result was to clear the German first position and the ground between Station Road and Beaucourt trench. At the same time the right battalion—which had been waiting outside Beaucourt for twenty-four hours—carried the place by

REPAIRING A CAPTURED GERMAN AEROPLANE

A MINE EXPLODING BEFORE THE ASSAULT

storm. Its commanding officer, Lieutenant-Colonel Freyberg, had been already three times wounded, but that morning he led the charge in person. Though wounded a fourth time most severely, he refused to lay down his command till he had placed posts with perfect military judgment to the east and north-east to prevent a surprise and had given full instructions to his successor. To his brilliant leadership the main achievement of the Naval Division was due.* His success is an instructive proof of the value of holding forward positions even though flanks and rear are threatened, if you are dealing with a shaken enemy and have a certainty of supports behind you. Troops who make a bold advance will, if they retire, have achieved nothing, and will certainly lose a large proportion of their strength. If they stay where they are they run the risk of being totally destroyed; but, on the other hand, there is a chance of completely turning the scale. For it should be remembered that an isolated detachment, if it has the enemy on its flank and rear, is itself on the flank and rear of the enemy, and the moral effect of its position may be the determining factor in breaking the enemy's resistance.

By the night of Tuesday, 14th November, our

---

* Colonel Freyberg had received the D.S.O. in Gallipoli for swimming ashore and lighting flares during the feint of landing in the Gulf of Saros on April 24-25, 1915. He received the Victoria Cross for the taking of Beaucourt. "The personality, valour, and utter contempt of danger on the part of this single officer," so ran the official announcement, "enabled the lodgement in the most advanced objectives of the corps to be permanently held, and on this *point d'appui* the line was eventually formed."

total of prisoners on the five-mile front of battle was well over 5,000—the largest captures yet made in the time by any army in the West since the campaign began. And the advance was not yet over The German counter-attack of the 15th failed to win back any ground. Just east of *Nov. 15.* Beaumont Hamel there was an extensive No Man's Land, for Munich trench could not be claimed by either side, but in the Beaucourt area we steadily pressed on. On Thursday, the 16th, we pushed east from Beaucourt village along *Nov. 16.* the north bank of the Ancre, establishing posts in the Bois d'Hollande to the north-west of Grandcourt. Frost had set in, and it was possible from the Thiepval ridge or from the slopes above Hamel to see clearly the whole new battlefield, and even in places to follow the infantry advance—a thing which had not been feasible since the summer fighting. By that day our total of prisoners was over 6,000. On the 17th we again advanced, and on Saturday, the 18th, in a downpour of icy *Nov. 18.* rain, the Canadians on the right of the Fifth Army, attacking from Regina trench, moved far down the slope towards the river, while the centre pushed close to the western skirts of Grandcourt.

It was the last attack, with which concluded the fourth stage of the Battle of the Somme. The weather now closed down like a curtain upon the drama. Though in modern war we may disregard the seasons, the elements take their revenge and armies are forced at a certain stage, whether they will it or not, into that trench warfare which takes the place of the winter quarters of Marlborough's

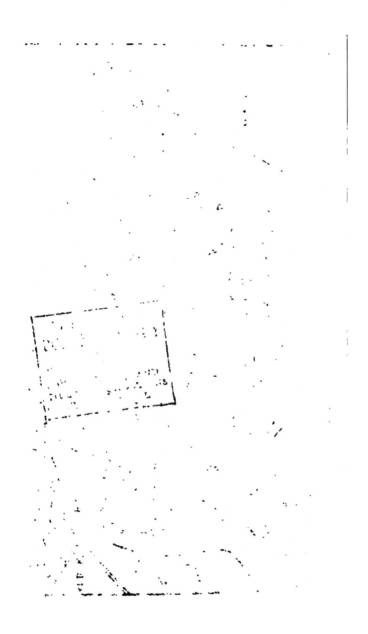

day. The Battle of the Ancre was a fitting *dénouement* to the great action. It gave us three strongly fortified villages, and practically the whole of the minor spur which runs from north of Beaumont Hamel to Beaucourt. It extended the breach in the main enemy position by five miles. Our front was now far down the slopes from the Thiepval ridge and north and west of Grandcourt. We had taken well over 7,000 prisoners and vast quantities of material, including several hundred machine guns. Our losses had been comparatively slight, while those of the enemy were—on his own admission—severe. Above all, just when he was beginning to argue himself into the belief that the Somme offensive was over we upset all his calculations by an unexpected stroke. We had opened the old wound and undermined his *moral* by reviving the terrors of the unknown and the unexpected.

We are still too close to events to attempt an estimate of the Battle of the Somme as a whole. It will be the task of later historians to present it in its true perspective. Even now one thing is clear. Before 1st July Verdun had been the greatest continuous battle fought in the world's history; but the Somme surpassed it both in numbers of men engaged, in the tactical difficulty of the objectives, and in its importance in the strategical scheme of the campaign. Calculations of the forces employed would for the present be indiscreet and estimates of casualties untrustworthy, but some idea of its significance may be gathered from the way in which it preoccupied the enemy High Command. It was the fashion in Germany to describe it as a futile attack upon an unshakable fortress, an attack which might be disregarded by her public opinion while she continued her true business of conquest in the East. But the fact remained that the great bulk of the German troops and by far the best of them were kept congregated in this area. In November Germany had 127 divisions on the Western front, and no more than seventy-five in the East. Though Brussilov's attack and von Falkenhayn's Rumanian expedition compelled her to send fresh troops eastward she did not diminish but increased her strength in the West. In June she had fourteen divisions on the Somme; in November she had in line or just out of it well over forty.

By what test are we to judge the result of a battle in modern war? In the old days of open fighting there was little room for doubt, since the retreat or rout or envelopment of the beaten army was too clear for argument. To-day, when the total battle-front is 3,000 miles, such easy proofs are lacking; but the principle remains the same. A battle is final when it ends in the destruction of the enemy's fighting strength. A battle is won—and it may be decisively won—when it results in achieving the strategic purpose of one of the combatants, provided that purpose is, on military grounds, a wise one. Hence the amount of territory occupied and the number of important points captured are not necessarily sound criteria at all. If they were, the German overrunning of Poland would have been a great victory, when, as a matter of fact, it was a failure. Von Hindenburg sought to destroy the Russian army, and the Russian army declined the honour. The success or defeat of a strategic purpose, that is the sole test. Judging by this, Tannenberg was a victory for Germany, the Marne for France, and the First Battle of Ypres for Britain. The Battle of the Somme was no less a victory since it achieved the purpose of the Allies.

In the first place, it relieved Verdun, and enabled Nivelle to advance presently to conspicuous victories. In the second place, it detained the main German forces on the Western front. In the third place, it drew into the battle, and gravely depleted, the surplus man-power of the enemy, and struck a shattering blow at his *moral*. For two years the German behind the shelter of his trench-works and the great engine of his artillery had fought with comparatively little cost against opponents far less well equipped. The Somme put the shoe on the other foot, and he came to know what the British learned at Ypres and the French in the Artois— what it felt like to be bombarded out of existence, and to cling to shell holes and the ruins of trenches under a pitiless fire. It was a new thing in his experience, and took the heart out of men who, under other conditions, had fought with skill and courage. Further, the Allies had dislocated his whole military machine. Their ceaseless pressure had crippled his Staff work, and confused the organisation of which he had justly boasted.

Sir Douglas Haig's sober summary is the last word on the subject. "The enemy's power has not yet been broken, nor is it yet possible to form an estimate of the time the war may last before the objects for which the Allies are fighting have been attained. But the Somme battle has placed beyond doubt the ability of the Allies to gain these objects.

The German army is the mainstay of the Central Powers, and a full half of that army, despite all the advantages of the defensive, supported by the strongest fortifications, suffered defeat on the Somme this year. Neither the victors nor the vanquished will forget this; and, though bad weather has given the enemy a respite, there will undoubtedly be many thousands in his ranks who will begin the new campaign with little confidence in their ability to resist our assaults or to overcome our defence."

Let it be freely granted that Germany met the strain in a soldierly fashion. As von Armin's report showed, she set herself at once to learn the lessons of the battle and to revise her methods where revision was needed. She made drastic changes in her High Commands. She endeavoured still further to exploit her already much-exploited man-power. She decreed a *levée-en-masse*, and combed out even from vital industries every man who was capable of taking the field. She swept the young and old into her ranks, and, as was said of Lee's army in its last campaign, she robbed the cradle and the grave. Her effort was magnificent—and it was war. She had created since 1st July some thirty odd new divisions, formed partly by converting garrison units into field troops, and partly by regrouping units from existing formations—taking a regiment away from a four-regiment division, and a battalion from a four-battalion regiment, and withdrawing the Jaeger battalions. But these changes, though they increased the number of her units, did not add proportionately to the aggregate of her numerical strength, and we may take 100,000 men as the maximum of the total gain in field troops from this readjustment. More-

over, she had to provide artillery and Staffs for each
of the new divisions, which involved a heavy strain
upon services already taxed to the full. We know
that her commissioned classes had been badly depleted. "The shortage," so ran an order of von
Hindenburg's in September, "due to our heavy casualties, of experienced, energetic, and well-trained
junior officers is sorely felt at the present time."

The Battle of the Somme had, therefore, fulfilled
the Allied purpose in taxing to the uttermost the German war machine. It tried the Command, it tried
the nation at home, and it tried to the last limit of
endurance the men in the line. The place became a
name of terror. Though belittled in *communiqués,*
and rarely mentioned in the Press, it was a word of
ill-omen to the whole German people, that "blood-
bath" to which many journeyed and from which few
returned. Of what avail their easy conquests on
the Danube when this deadly cancer in the West was
eating into the vitals of the nation? Winter might
give a short respite—though the Battle of the Ancre
had been fought in winter weather—but spring
would come, and the evil would grow malignant
again. Germany gathered herself for a great
effort, marshalling for compulsory war work the
whole male population between seventeen and sixty,
sending every man to the trenches who could
walk on sound feet, doling out food supplies on the
minimum scale for the support of life, and making
desperate efforts by submarine warfare to cripple
her enemies' strength. But what if her enemies followed her example? The Allies lagged far behind
her in their adoption of drastic remedies and even so
they had won to an equality and more than an equal-

ity in battle power. What if they also took the final
step? They had shown that they had no thought
of peace except at their own dictation. They had
willed the end; what if they also willed the ultimate
means?

In November, behind the rodomontade of German
journalists over Rumanian victories and the stout
words of German statesmen, it was easy to dis-
cern a profound and abiding anxiety. Let us
take two quotations from a heavily censored Press.
The *Leipsiger Neueste Nachrichten* wrote: "We
realise now that England is our real enemy, and that
she is prepared to do everything in her power to
conquer us. She has gone so far as to introduce
compulsory service to attain her aims. Let us recognise her strength of purpose, and take the necessary
precautions. It is more than probable that, if the
lack of war material and supplies does not put a stop
to the Battle of the Somme, she will not abandon
her plans. On the contrary, she will make use of
the winter to accumulate immense reserves of ammunition. There is no doubt as to her having the
money necessary, and it would be foolish optimism
on our part to imagine that the terrible fighting on
the Western front will not start again next spring."
And this from the *Berliner Lokalanzeiger*: "We
recognise that the whole war to-day is, in the main,
a question of labour resources, and England has
taken the lead in welding together all such resources.
Thanks to her immense achievement in this sphere,
our most dangerous enemy has arrived at a position
in which she is able to set enormous weapons against
us. It is the Battle of the Somme above all that
teaches us this."

DEVASTATION—"SOMEWHERE IN FRANCE"

EVENING BEHIND THE LINES

In every great action there is a major purpose, a reasoned and calculated purpose which takes no account of the accidents of fortune. But in most actions there come sudden strokes of luck which turn the scale. For such strokes a general has a right to hope, but on them he dare not build. Marengo, Waterloo, Chancellorsville—most of the great battles of older times—showed these good gifts of destiny. But in the elaborate and mechanical warfare of to-day they come rarely, and at the Battle of the Somme they did not fall to the lot of the British Commander-in-Chief. He did what he set out to do; step by step he drove his way through the German defences; but it was all done by hard and stubborn fighting, without any bounty from capricious fortune. The Germans had claimed that their line was impregnable; we broke it again and again. They had counted on their artillery machine; we crippled and outmatched it. They had decried the fighting stuff of our new armies; we showed that it was more than a match for their Guards and Brandenburgers.* All these things we did, soberly, patiently, after the British fashion. Our major purpose was attained. Like some harsh and remorseless chemical, the waxing Allied energy was eating into the German waning mass. There was thought and care in the plan, and that resolution which is so strong that it can dare to be patient. The guarantee of the continuity of the Allied effort was its orderly progress. The heroic dash may fail

* Between 1st July and 18th November the British on the Somme took just over 38,000 prisoners, including 800 officers, 29 heavy guns, 96 field guns, 136 trench mortars, and 514 machine guns.

and be shattered by the counter-attack, but this sure
and methodical pressure had the inevitability of a
natural law. It was attrition, but attrition in the
acute form—not like the slow erosion of cliffs by the
sea, but like the steady crumbling of a mountain to
which hydraulic engineers have applied a mighty
head of water.

The fall of winter, with its storms and sodden
ground and brief hours of daylight, marked the
close of a stage, but not of the battle. Advances
might be fewer, the territory gained might be less,
but the offensive did not slacken. Still on a broad
front the Allied pressure was continuously maintained by means of their artillery and other services,
and the sapping of the enemy's strength went on
without ceasing. The hardships of winter would
be felt more acutely by forces which had been outmatched in the long five months' battle; for it is
a law of life and of war that the weakness of the less
strong grows *pari passu* with the power of the
stronger. Those who judged of success only by the
ground occupied might grow restive during those
days of apparent inaction, but the soldier knew that
they represented blows struck at the enemy which
were not less deadly in effect than a spectacular advance. The major purpose was still proceeding.

A sketch of the main features of a great action
is like the rough outline of a picture before the
artist has added the colours and the proportions of
life. It cannot even hint at the rich human quality
of it all, the staunch brotherhood in arms, the faith-
fulness, the cheerful sacrifice, the fortitude, any
more than it can portray the terror and suffering.

But it is well to realise that this battle, unparalleled
in its magnitude and gravity, was also unique in
another circumstance. It was the effort of the whole
British nation, and an effort made of each man's
free will. Her armies were not a separate caste,
whose doings the ordinary citizen watched with interest and excitement but with a certain detachment,
as those of friendly gladiators hired for a purpose
foreign to the decent routine of his life. They were
composed of the ordinary citizen himself. The
Army was the people. Not a class or profession
or trade but had sent its tens of thousands to the
ranks, and scarcely a British home but had losses
to mourn. Those fighting men had come willingly
to the task, because their own interest and happiness
were become one with their country's victory.
Having willed the end, they willed also the means,
and showed themselves gluttons for the full rigour
of service. The riddle which Lincoln propounded
had been nobly answered.

No great thing is achieved without a price, and
on the Somme fell the very flower of our race, the
straightest of limb, the keenest of brain, the most
eager of spirit. In such a mourning each man
thinks first of his friends. Each of us has seen his
crowded circle become like the stalls of a theatre at
an unpopular play. Each has suddenly found the
world of time strangely empty and eternity strangely
thronged. To look back upon the gallant procession of those who offered their all and had their gift
accepted, is to know exultation as well as sorrow.
The young men who died almost before they had
gazed on the world, the makers and the doers who
left their tasks unfinished, were greater in their

deaths than in their lives. They builded better than they knew, for the sum of their imperfections was made perfect, and out of loss they won for their country and mankind an enduring gain. Their memory will abide so long as men are found to set honour before ease, and a nation lives not for its ledgers alone but for some purpose of virtue. They have become, in the fancy of Henry Vaughan, the shining spires of that City to which we travel.

'APPENDIX I

SIR DOUGLAS HAIG'S SECOND DISPATCH

WAR OFFICE, *29th December* 1916.

The following Dispatch has been received by the Secretary of State for War from General Sir Douglas Haig, G.C.B., Commanding-in-Chief, the British Forces in France:—

General Headquarters,
23rd December 1916.

MY LORD,

I have the honour to submit the following report on the operations of the Forces under my Command since the 19th May, the date of my last Dispatch.

1. The principle of an offensive campaign during the summer of 1916 had already been decided on by all the Allies. The various possible alternatives on the Western front had been studied and discussed by General Joffre and myself, and we were in complete agreement as to the front to be attacked by the combined French and British Armies. Preparations for our offensive had made considerable progress; but as the date on which the attack should begin was dependent on many doubtful factors, a final decision on that point was deferred until the general situation should become clearer.

Subject to the necessity of commencing operations before the summer was too far advanced, and with due regard to the general situation, I desired to postpone my attack as long as possible. The British Armies were growing in numbers and the supply of munitions was steadily increasing. Moreover, a very large proportion of the officers and men under my command were still far from being fully trained, and the longer the attack could be deferred the more efficient they would become. On the other hand the Germans were continuing to press their attacks at Verdun, and both there and on the Italian front, where the Austrian offensive was gaining ground, it was evident that the strain might become too great to be borne unless timely action were taken to relieve it. Accordingly, while maintaining constant touch with General Joffre in regard to all these considerations, my preparations were pushed on, and I agreed, with the consent of H.M. Government, that my attack should be launched whenever the general situation required it with as great a force as I might then be able to make available.

2. By the end of May the pressure of the enemy on the Italian front had assumed such serious proportions that the Russian campaign was opened early in June, and the brilliant successes gained by our Allies against the Austrians at once caused a movement of German troops from the Western to the Eastern front. This, however, did not lessen the pressure on Verdun. The heroic defence of our French Allies had already gained many weeks of inestimable value and had caused the enemy very heavy losses; but the strain continued to increase. In view, therefore, of the situation in the various theatres of war, it was eventually agreed between General Joffre and myself that the combined French and British offensive should not be postponed beyond the end of June.

The British Objective

The object of that offensive was threefold:
   (i.) To relieve the pressure on Verdun.
   (ii.) To assist our Allies in the other theatres of war

by stopping any further transfer of German troops from the Western front.

(iii.) To wear down the strength of the forces opposed to us.

3. While my final preparations were in progress the enemy made two unsuccessful attempts to interfere with my arrangements. The first, directed on the 21st May against our positions on the Vimy Ridge, south and south-east of Souchez, resulted in a small enemy gain of no strategic or tactical importance; and rather than weaken my offensive by involving additional troops in the task of recovering the lost ground, I decided to consolidate a position in rear of our original line.

The second enemy attack was delivered on the 2nd June on a front of over one and a half miles from Mount Sorrell to Hooge, and succeeded in penetrating to a maximum depth of 700 yards. As the southern part of the lost position commanded our trenches, I judged it necessary to recover it, and by an attack launched on the 13th June, carefully prepared and well executed, this was successfully accomplished by the troops on the spot.

Neither of these enemy attacks succeeded in delaying the preparations for the major operations which I had in view.

4. These preparations were necessarily very elaborate and took considerable time.

Vast stocks of ammunition and stores of all kinds had to be accumulated beforehand within a convenient distance of our front. To deal with these many miles of new railways—both standard and narrow gauge—and trench tramways were laid. All available roads were improved, many others were made, and long causeways were. built over marshy valleys. Many additional dug-outs had to be provided as shelter for the troops, for use as dressing stations for the wounded, and as magazines for storing ammunition, food, water, and engineering material. Scores of miles of deep communication trenches had to be dug, as well as trenches for telephone wires, assembly and assault trenches, and numerous gun emplacements and observation posts.

Important mining operations were undertaken, and charges were laid at various points beneath the enemy's lines.

Except in the river valleys, the existing supplies of water were hopelessly insufficient to meet the requirements of the numbers of men and horses to be concentrated in this area as the preparations for our offensive proceeded. To meet this difficulty many wells and borings were sunk, and over one hundred pumping plants were installed. More than one hundred and twenty miles of water mains were laid, and everything was got ready to ensure an adequate water supply as our troops advanced.

Much of this preparatory work had to be done under very trying conditions, and was liable to constant interruption from the enemy's fire. The weather, on the whole, was bad, and the local accommodation totally insufficient for housing the troops employed, who consequently had to content themselves with such rough shelter as could be provided in the circumstances. All this labour, too, had to be carried out in addition to fighting and to the everyday work of maintaining existing defences. It threw a very heavy strain on the troops, which was borne by them with a cheerfulness beyond all praise.

The German Position

5. The enemy's position to be attacked was of a very formidable character, situated on a high, undulating tract of ground, which rises to more than 500 feet above sea-level, and forms the watershed between the Somme on the one side and the rivers of south-western Belgium on the other. On the southern face of this watershed, the general trend of which is from east-south-east to west-north-west, the ground falls in a series of long irregular spurs and deep depressions to the valley of the Somme. Well down the forward slopes

of this face the enemy's first system of defence, starting from the Somme near Curlu, ran at first northwards for 3,000 yards, then westwards for 7,000 yards to near Fricourt, where it turned nearly due north, forming a great salient angle in the enemy's line.

Some 10,000 yards north of Fricourt the trenches crossed the River Ancre, a tributary of the Somme, and still running northwards passed over the summit of the watershed, about Hebuterne and Gommecourt, and then down its northern spurs to Arras.

On the 20,000 yards front between the Somme and the Ancre the enemy had a strong second system of defence, sited generally on or near the southern crest of the highest part of the watershed, at an average distance of from 3,000 to 5,000 yards behind his first system of trenches.

During nearly two years' preparation he had spared no pains to render these defences impregnable. The first and second systems each consisted of several lines of deep trenches, well provided with bomb-proof shelters and with numerous communication trenches connecting them. The front of the trenches in each system was protected by wire entanglements, many of them in two belts forty yards broad, built of iron stakes interlaced with barbed wire, often almost as thick as a man's finger.

The numerous woods and villages in and between these systems of defence had been turned into veritable fortresses. The deep cellars usually to be found in the villages, and the numerous pits and quarries common to a chalk country, were used to provide cover for machine guns and trench mortars. The existing cellars were supplemented by elaborate dug-outs, sometimes in two storeys, and these were connected up by passages as much as thirty feet below the surface of the ground. The salients in the enemy's line, from which he could bring enfilade fire across his front, were made into self-contained forts, and often protected by mine fields; while strong redoubts and concrete machine gun emplacements had been constructed in positions from which he could sweep

his own trenches should these be taken. The ground
lent itself to good artillery observation on the enemy's
part, and he had skilfully arranged for cross fire by his
guns.

These various systems of defence, with the fortified localities and other supporting points between them, were cun-
ningly sited to afford each other mutual assistance and to
admit of the utmost possible development of enfilade and
flanking fire by machine guns and artillery. They formed,
in short, not merely a series of successive lines, but one com-
posite system of enormous depth and strength.

Behind his second system of trenches, in addition to
woods, villages and other strong points prepared for defence,
the enemy had several other lines already completed; and
we had learned from aeroplane reconnaissance that he was
hard at work improving and strengthening these and digging
fresh ones between them and still further back.

In the area above described, between the Somme and
the Ancre, our front line trenches ran parallel and close to
those of the enemy, but below them. We had good direct
observation on his front system of trenches and on the various
defences sited on the slopes above us between his first and
second systems; but the second system itself, in many
places, could not be observed from the ground in our possession, while, except from the air, nothing could be seen of
his more distant defences.

North of the Ancre, where the opposing trenches ran
transversely across the main ridge, the enemy's defences were
equally elaborate and formidable. So far as command of
ground was concerned, we were here practically on level
terms; but, partly as a result of this, our direct observation
over the ground held by the enemy was not so good as it
was further south. On portions of this front, the opposing
first line trenches were more widely separated from each
other; while in the valleys to the north were many hidden
gun positions from which the enemy could develop flanking
fire on our troops as they advanced across the open.

THE THREE PHASES

6. The period of active operations dealt with in this dispatch divides itself roughly into three phases. The first phase opened with the attack of the 1st July, the success of which evidently came as a surprise to the enemy and caused considerable confusion and disorganisation in his ranks. The advantages gained on that date and developed during the first half of July may be regarded as having been rounded off by the operations of the 14th July and three following days, which gave us possession of the southern crest of the main plateau between Delville Wood and Bazentin-le-Petit.

We then entered upon a contest lasting for many weeks, during which the enemy, having found his strongest defences unavailing, and now fully alive to his danger, put forth his utmost efforts to keep his hold on the main ridge. This stage of the battle constituted a prolonged and severe struggle for mastery between the contending armies, in which, although progress was slow and difficult, the confidence of our troops in their ability to win was never shaken. Their tenacity and determination proved more than equal to their task, and by the first week in September they had established a fighting superiority that has left its mark on the enemy, of which possession of the ridge was merely the visible proof.

The way was then opened for the third phase, in which our advance was pushed down the forward slopes of the ridge and further extended on both flanks until, from Morval to Thiepval, the whole plateau and a good deal of ground beyond were in our possession. Meanwhile our gallant Allies, in addition to great successes south of the Somme, had pushed their advance, against equally determined opposition, and under most difficult tactical conditions, up the long slopes on our immediate right, and were now preparing to drive the enemy from the summit of the narrow and difficult portion of the main ridge which lies between the Combles Valley and the River Tortille, a stream flowing from the north into the Somme just below Peronne.

7. Defences of the nature described could only be attacked with any prospect of success after careful artillery preparation. It was accordingly decided that our bombardment should begin on the 24th June; and a large force of artillery was brought into action for the purpose.

Artillery bombardments were also carried out daily at different points on the rest of our front, and during the period from the 24th June to 1st July gas was discharged with good effect at more than forty places along our line upon a frontage which in total amounted to over 15 miles. Some 70 raids, too, were undertaken by our infantry between Gommecourt and our extreme left north of Ypres during the week preceding the attack, and these kept me well informed as to the enemy's dispositions, besides serving other useful purposes.

On the 25th June the Royal Flying Corps carried out a general attack on the enemy's observation balloons, destroying nine of them, and depriving the enemy for the time being of this form of observation.

The First Stage

8. On July 1st, at 7.30 a.m., after a final hour of exceptionally violent bombardment, our infantry assault was launched. Simultaneously the French attacked on both sides of the Somme, co-operating closely with us.

The British main front of attack extended from Maricourt on our right, round the salient at Fricourt, to the Ancre in front of St. Pierre Divion. To assist this main attack by holding the enemy's reserves and occupying his artillery, the enemy's trenches north of the Ancre, as far as Serre inclusive, were to be assaulted simultaneously; while further north a subsidiary attack was to be made on both sides of the salient at Gommecourt.

I had entrusted the attack on the front from Maricourt to Serre to the Fourth Army, under the command of General Sir Henry S. Rawlinson, Bart., K.C.B., K.C.V.O., with five Army Corps at his disposal. The subsidiary attack at Gomme-court was carried out by troops from the Army commanded by General Sir E. H. H. Allenby, K.C.B.

Just prior to the attack the mines which had been prepared under the enemy's lines were exploded, and smoke was discharged at many places along our front. Through this smoke our infantry advanced to the attack with the utmost steadiness, in spite of the very heavy barrage of the enemy's guns. On our right our troops met with immediate success, and rapid progress was made. Before midday Montauban had been carried, and shortly afterwards the Briqueterie, to the east, and the whole of the ridge to the west of the village were in our hands. Opposite Mametz part of our assembly trenches had been practically levelled by the enemy artillery, making it necessary for our infantry to advance to the attack across 400 yards of open ground. None the less they forced their way into Mametz, and reached their objective in the valley beyond, first throwing out a defensive flank towards Fricourt on their left. At the same time the enemy's trenches were entered north of Fricourt, so that the enemy's garrison in that village was pressed on three sides. Further north, though the villages of La Boisselle and Ovillers for the time being resisted our attack, our troops drove deeply into the German lines on the flanks of these strongholds, and so paved the way for their capture later. On the spur running south from Thiepval the work known as the Leipzig Salient was stormed, and severe fighting took place for the possession of the village and its defences. Here and north of the valley of the Ancre as far as Serre, on the left flank of our attack, our initial successes were not sustained. Striking progress was made at many points, and parties of troops penetrated the enemy's positions to the outer defences of Grandcourt, and also to Pendant Copse and Serre; but the enemy's continued resistance at Thiepval and Beaumont Hamel made it impossible to forward reinforcements and ammunition, and, in spite of their gallant efforts, our troops were forced to withdraw during the night to their own lines.

The subsidiary attack at Gommecourt also forced its way into the enemy's positions; but there met with such vigorous opposition, that as soon as it was considered that the attack had fulfilled its object our troops were withdrawn.

9. In view of the general situation at the end of the first day's operations, I decided that the best course was to press forward on a front extending from our junction with the French to a point halfway between La Boisselle and Contalmaison, and to limit the offensive on our left for the present to a slow and methodical advance. North of the Ancre such preparations were to be made as would hold the enemy to his positions, and enable the attack to be resumed there later if desirable. In order that General Sir Henry Rawlinson might be left free to concentrate his attention on the portion of the front where the attack was to be pushed home, I also decided to place the operations against the front, La Boisselle to Serre, under the command of General Sir Hubert de la P. Gough, K.C.B., to whom I accordingly allotted the two northern corps of Sir Henry Rawlinson's army. My instructions to Sir Hubert Gough were that his Army was to maintain a steady pressure on the front from La Boisselle to the Serre Road, and to act as a pivot, on which our line could swing as our attacks on his right made progress towards the north.

10. During the succeeding days the attack was continued on these lines. In spite of strong counter-attacks on the Briqueterie and Montauban, by midday on the 2nd July our troops had captured Fricourt, and in the afternoon and evening stormed Fricourt Wood and the farm to the north. During the 3rd and 4th July Bernafay and Caterpillar Woods were also captured, and our troops pushed forward to the railway north of Mametz. On these days the reduction of La Boisselle was completed after hard fighting, while the outskirts of Contalmaison were reached on the 5th July. North

of La Boisselle also the enemy's forces opposite us were kept constantly engaged; and our holding in the Leipzig Salient was gradually increased.

To sum up the results of the fighting of these five days, on a front of over six miles, from the Briqueterie to La Boisselle, our troops had swept over the whole of the enemy's first and strongest system of defence, which he had done his utmost to render impregnable. They had driven him back over a distance of more than a mile, and had carried four elaborately fortified villages.

The number of prisoners passed back at the close of the 5th July had already reached the total of ninety-four officers and 5,724 other ranks.

THE RESULT OF FIVE DAYS

11. After the five days' heavy and continuous fighting just described it was essential to carry out certain readjustments and reliefs of the forces engaged. In normal conditions of enemy resistance the amount of progress that can be made at any time without a pause in the general advance is necessarily limited. Apart from the physical exhaustion of the attacking troops and the considerable distances separating the enemy's successive main systems of defence, special artillery preparation was required before a successful assault could be delivered. Meanwhile, however, local operations were continued in spite of much unfavourable weather. The attack on Contalmaison and Mametz Wood was undertaken on the 7th July, and after three days' obstinate fighting, in the course of which the enemy delivered several powerful counter-attacks, the village and the whole of the wood, except its northern border, were finally secured. On the 7th July also a footing was gained in the outer defences of Ovillers, while on the 9th July on our extreme right Maltz Horn Farm—an important point on the spur north of Hardecourt—was secured.

A thousand yards north of this farm our troops had suc-

ceeded at the second attempt in establishing themselves on
the 8th July in the southern end of Trones Wood.   The
enemy's positions in the northern and eastern parts of this
wood were very strong, and no less than eight powerful
German counter-attacks were made here during the next
five days.   In the course of this struggle portions of the
wood changed hands several times; but we were left eventually, on the 13th July, in possession of the southern part of it.

12. Meanwhile Mametz Wood had been entirely cleared
of the enemy, and with Trones Wood also practically in our
possession we were in a position to undertake an assault
upon the enemy's second system of defences.   Arrangements
were accordingly made for an attack to be delivered at daybreak on the morning of the 14th July against a front extending from Longueval to Bazentin-le-Petit Wood, both
inclusive.   Contalmaison Villa, on a spur 1,000 yards west
of Bazentin-le-Petit Wood, had already been captured to
secure the left flank of the attack, and advantage had been
taken of the progress made by our infantry to move our
artillery forward into new positions.   The preliminary bombardment had opened on the 11th July.   The opportunities
offered by the ground for enfilading the enemy's lines were
fully utilised and did much to secure the success of our attack.

13. In the early hours of the 14th July the attacking
troops moved out over the open for a distance of from about
1,000 to 1,400 yards, and lined up in the darkness just below
the crest and some 300 to 500 yards from the enemy's trenches.
Their advance was covered by strong patrols, and their correct deployment had been ensured by careful previous preparations.   The whole movement was carried out unobserved
and without touch being lost in any case.   The decision to
attempt a night operation of this magnitude with an Army,
the bulk of which has been raised since the beginning of the
war, was perhaps the highest tribute that could be paid to
the quality of our troops.   It would not have been possible
but for the most careful preparation and forethought, as well
as thorough reconnaissance of the ground, which was in

many cases made personally by Divisional, Brigade and Battalion Commanders and their staffs before framing their detailed orders for the advance.

The Second Stage

The actual assault was delivered at 3.25 a.m. on the 14th July, when there was just sufficient light to be able to distinguish friend from foe at short ranges, and along the whole front attacked our troops, preceded by a very effective artillery barrage, swept over the enemy's first trenches and on into the defences beyond.

On our right the enemy was driven from his last foothold in Trones Wood, and by 8.0 a.m. we had cleared the whole of it, relieving a body of 170 men who had maintained themselves all night in the northern corner of the wood, although completely surrounded by the enemy. Our position in the wood was finally consolidated, and strong patrols were sent out from it in the direction of Guillemont and Longueval. The southern half of this latter village was already in the hands of our troops who had advanced west of Trones Wood. The northern half, with the exception of two strong points, was captured by 4.0 p.m. after a severe struggle.

In the centre of our attack Bazentin-le-Grand village and wood were also gained, and our troops pushing northwards captured Bazentin-le-Petit village, and the cemetery to the east. Here the enemy counter-attacked twice about midday without success, and again in the afternoon, on the latter occasion momentarily reoccupying the northern half of the village as far as the church. Our troops immediately returned to the attack, and drove him out again with heavy losses. To the left of the village Bazentin-le-Petit Wood was cleared, in spite of the considerable resistance of the enemy along its western edge, where we successfully repulsed a counter-attack. In the afternoon further ground was gained to the west of the Wood, and posts were established immediately south of Pozieres.

The enemy's troops, who had been severely handled in these attacks and counter-attacks, began to show signs of disorganisation, and it was reported early in the afternoon that it was possible to advance to High Wood. General Rawlinson, who had held a force of cavalry in readiness for such an eventuality, decided to employ a part of it. As the fight progressed small bodies of this force had pushed forward gradually, keeping in close touch with the development of the action and prepared to seize quickly any opportunity that might occur. A squadron now came up on the flanks of our infantry, who entered High Wood at about 8.0 p.m., and, after some hand-to-hand fighting, cleared the whole of the Wood with the exception of the northern apex. Acting mounted in co-operation with the infantry the cavalry came into action with good effect, killing several of the enemy and capturing some prisoners.

14. On the 15th July the battle still continued, though on a reduced scale. Arrow Head Copse, between the southern edge of Trones Wood and Guillemont, and Waterlot Farm, on the Longueval-Guillemont Road, were seized, and Delville Wood was captured and held against several hostile counter-attacks. In Longueval fierce fighting continued until dusk for the possession of the two strong points and the orchards to the north of the village. The situation in this area made the position of our troops in High Wood somewhat precarious, and they now began to suffer numerous casualties from the enemy's heavy shelling. Accordingly orders were given for their withdrawal, and this was effected during the night of the 15-16th July without interference by the enemy. All the wounded were brought in.

In spite of repeated enemy counter-attacks further progress was made on the night of the 16th July along the enemy's main second line trenches north-west of Bazentin-le-Petit Wood to within 500 yards of the north-east corner of the village of Pozieres, which our troops were already approaching from the South.

Meanwhile the operations further north had also made progress. Since the attack of the 7th July the enemy in and about Ovillers had been pressed relentlessly, and gradually driven back by incessant bombing attacks and local assaults, in accordance with the general instructions I had given to General Sir Hubert Gough. On the 16th July a large body of the garrison of Ovillers surrendered, and that night and during the following day, by a direct advance from the west across No Man's Land, our troops carried the remainder of the village and pushed out along the spur to the north and eastwards towards Pozieres.

15. The results of the operations of the 14th July and subsequent days were of considerable importance. The enemy's second main system of defence had been captured on a front of over three miles. We had again forced him back more than a mile, and had gained possession of the southern crest of the main ridge on a front of 6,000 yards. Four more of his fortified villages and three woods had been wrested from him by determined fighting, and our advanced troops had penetrated as far as his third line of defence. In spite of a resolute resistance and many counter-attacks, in which the enemy had suffered severely, our line was definitely established from Maltz Horn Farm, where we met the French left, northwards along the eastern edge of Trones Wood to Longueval, then westwards past Bazentin-le-Grand to the northern corner of Bazentin-le-Petit and Bazentin-le-Petit Wood, and then westwards again past the southern face of Pozieres to the north of Ovillers. Posts were established at Arrow Head Copse and Waterlot Farm, while we had troops thrown forward in Delville Wood and towards High Wood, though their position was not yet secure.

I cannot speak too highly of the skill, daring, endurance and determination by which these results had been achieved. Great credit is due to Sir Henry Rawlinson for the thoroughness and care with which this difficult undertaking was planned; while the advance and deployment made by night without confusion, and the complete success of the subsequent attack, constitute a striking tribute to the discipline and spirit of the troops engaged, as well as to the powers of leadership and organisation of their commanders and staffs.

During these operations and their development on the 15th a number of enemy guns were taken, making our total captures since the 1st July 8 heavy howitzers, 4 heavy guns, 42 field and light guns and field howitzers, 30 trench mortars and 52 machine guns. Very considerable losses had been inflicted on the enemy, and the prisoners captured amounted to over 2,000, bringing the total since the 1st July to over 10,000.

The New Situation

16. There was strong evidence that the enemy forces engaged on the battle front had been severely shaken by the repeated successes gained by ourselves and our Allies; but the great strength and depth of his defences had secured for him sufficient time to bring up fresh troops, and he had still many powerful fortifications, both trenches, villages and woods, to which he could cling in our front and on our flanks.

We had, indeed, secured a footing on the main ridge, but only on a front of 6,000 yards; and desirous though I was to follow up quickly the successes we had won, it was necessary first to widen this front.

West of Bazentin-le-Petit the villages of Pozieres and Thiepval, together with the whole elaborate system of trenches round, between and on the main ridge behind them, had still to be carried. An advance further east would, however, eventually turn these defences, and all that was for the present required on the left flank of our attack was a steady, methodical, step by step advance as already ordered.

On our right flank the situation called for stronger measures. At Delville Wood and Longueval our lines formed a sharp salient, from which our front ran on the one side westwards to Pozieres, and on the other southwards to Maltz Horn Farm. At Maltz Horn Farm our lines joined the French, and the Allied front continued still southwards to the village of Hem on the Somme.

This pronounced salient invited counter-attacks by the enemy. He possessed direct observation on it all round from Guillemont on the south-east to High Wood on the north-west. He could bring a concentric fire of artillery to bear not only on the wood and village, but also on the confined space behind, through which ran the French communications as well as ours, where great numbers of guns, besides ammunition and impedimenta of all sorts, had necessarily to be crowded together. Having been in occupation of this ground for nearly two years he knew every foot of it, and could not fail to appreciate the possibilities of causing us heavy loss there by indirect artillery fire; while it was evident that if he could drive in the salient in our line and so gain direct observation on to the ground behind, our position in that area would become very uncomfortable.

If there had not been good grounds for confidence that the enemy was not capable of driving from this position troops who had shown themselves able to wrest it from him, the situation would have been an anxious one. In any case it was clear that the first requirement at the moment was that our right flank, and the French troops in extension of it, should swing up into line with our centre. To effect this, however, strong enemy positions had to be captured both by ourselves and by our Allies.

From Delville Wood the main plateau extends for 4,000 yards east-north-east to Les Bœufs and Morval, and for about the same distance south-eastwards to Leuze and Bouleaux Woods, which stand above and about 1,000 yards to the west of Combles. To bring my right up into line with the rest of my front it was necessary to capture Guillemont, Falfemont Farm and Leuze Wood, and then Ginchy and Bouleaux Wood. These localities were naturally very strong, and they had been elaborately fortified. The enemy's main

second line system of defence ran in front of them from Waterlot Farm, which was already in our hands, south-eastwards
to Falfemont Farm, and thence southwards to the Somme.
The importance of holding us back in this area could not
escape the enemy's notice, and he had dug and wired many
new trenches, both in front of and behind his original lines.
He had also brought up fresh troops, and there was no possibility of taking him by surprise.

The task before us was therefore a very difficult one and
entailed a real trial of strength between the opposing forces.
At this juncture its difficulties were increased by unfavourable
weather. The nature of the ground limited the possibility
of direct observation by our artillery fire, and we were consequently much dependent on observation from the air. As
in that element we had attained almost complete superiority,
all that we required was a clear atmosphere; but with this
we were not favoured for several weeks. We had rather
more rain than is usual in July and August, and even when
no rain fell there was an almost constant haze and frequent
low clouds.

The Swinging up of the Flanks

In swinging up my own right it was very important that
the French line north of the Somme should be advanced at
the same time in close combination with the movement of
the British troops. The line of demarcation agreed on
between the French commander and myself ran from Maltz
Horn Farm due eastwards to the Combles Valley and then
north-eastwards up that valley to a point midway between
Sailly-Saillisel and Morval. These two villages had been
fixed upon as the objectives, respectively, of the French left
and of my right. In order to advance in co-operation with
my right, and eventually to reach Sailly-Saillisel, our Allies
had still to fight their way up that portion of the main ridge
which lies between the Combles Valley on the west and the

River Tortille on the east. To do so they had to capture, in the first place, the strongly fortified villages of Maurepas, Le Forest, Rancourt, and Fregicourt, besides many woods and strong systems of trenches. As the high ground on each side of the Combles Valley commands the slopes of the ridge on the opposite side, it was essential that the advance of the two armies should be simultaneous and made in the closest co-operation. This was fully recognized by both armies, and our plans were made accordingly.

To carry out the necessary preparations to deal with the difficult situation outlined above a short pause was necessary to enable tired troops to be relieved and guns to be moved forward; while at the same time old communications had to be improved and new ones made. Entrenchments against probable counter-attacks could not be neglected, and fresh dispositions of troops were required for the new attacks to be directed eastwards.

It was also necessary to continue such pressure on the rest of our front, not only on the Ancre but further south, as would make it impossible for the enemy to devote himself entirely to resisting the advance between Delville Wood and the Somme. In addition it was desirable further to secure our hold on the main ridge west of Delville Wood by gaining more ground to our front in that direction. Orders were therefore issued in accordance with the general considerations explained above, and, without relaxing pressure along the enemy's front from Delville Wood to the West, preparations for an attack on Guillemont were pushed on.

17. During the afternoon of the 18th July the enemy developed his expected counter-attack against Delville Wood, after heavy preliminary shelling. By sheer weight of numbers and at very heavy cost he forced his way through the northern and north-eastern portions of the wood and into the northern half of Longueval, which our troops had cleared only that morning. In the south-east corner of the wood he was held up by a gallant defence, and further south three attacks on our positions in Waterlot Farm failed.

This enemy attack on Delville Wood marked the commencement of the long closely contested struggle which was not finally decided in our favour till the fall of Guillemont on the 3rd September, a decision which was confirmed by the capture of Ginchy six days later. Considerable gains were indeed made during this period; but progress was slow and bought only by hard fighting. A footing was established in High Wood on the 20th July and our line linked up thence with Longueval. A subsequent advance by the Fourth Army on the 23rd July on a wide front from Guillemont to near Pozieres found the enemy in great strength all along the line, with machine guns and forward troops in shell holes and newly constructed trenches well in front of his main defences. Although ground was won the strength of the resistance experienced showed that the hostile troops had recovered from their previous confusion sufficiently to necessitate long and careful preparation before further successes on any great scale could be secured.

An assault delivered simultaneously on this date by General Gough's Army against Pozieres gained considerable results, and by the morning of the 25th July the whole of that village was carried, including the cemetery, and important progress was made along the enemy's trenches to the north-east. That evening, after heavy artillery preparation, the enemy launched two more powerful counter-attacks, the one directed against our new position in and around High Wood and the other delivered from the north-west of Delville Wood. Both attacks were completely broken up with very heavy losses to the enemy.

On the 27th July the remainder of Delville Wood was recovered, and two days later the northern portion of Longueval and the orchards were cleared of the enemy, after severe fighting, in which our own and the enemy's artillery were very active.

18. On the 30th July the village of Guillemont and Falfemont Farm to the south-east were attacked, in conjunction with a French attack north of the Somme. A battalion

entered Guillemont, and part of it passed through to the far side; but as the battalions on either flank did not reach their objectives, it was obliged to fall back, after holding out for some hours on the western edge of the village. In a subsequent local attack on the 7th August our troops again entered Guillemont, but were again compelled to fall back owing to the failure of a simultaneous effort against the enemy's trenches on the flanks of the village.

The ground to the south of Guillemont was dominated by the enemy's positions in and about that village. It was therefore hoped that these positions might be captured first, before an advance to the south of them in the direction of Falfemont Farm was pushed further forward. It had now become evident, however, that Guillemont could not be captured as an isolated enterprise without very heavy loss, and, accordingly, arrangements were made with the French Army on our immediate right for a series of combined attacks, to be delivered in progressive stages, which should embrace Maurepas, Falfemont Farm, Guillemont, Leuze Wood and Ginchy.

An attempt on the 16th August to carry out the first stage of the pre-arranged scheme met with only partial success, and two days later, after a preliminary bombardment, lasting thirty-six hours, a larger combined attack was undertaken. In spite of a number of enemy counter-attacks—the most violent of which, levelled at the point of junction of the British with the French, succeeded in forcing our Allies and ourselves back from a part of the ground won—very valuable progress was made, and our troops established themselves in the outskirts of Guillemont village and occupied Guillemont Station. A violent counter-attack on Guillemont Station was repulsed on the 23rd August, and next day further important progress was made on a wide front north and east of Delville Wood.

19. Apart from the operations already described, others of a minor character, yet involving much fierce and obstinate fighting, continued during this period on the fronts of both

the British Armies. Our lines were pushed forward wherever possible by means of local attacks and by bombing and
sapping, and the enemy was driven out of various forward
positions from which he might hamper our progress.   By
these means many gains were made which, though small in
themselves, in the aggregate represented very considerable
advances.   In this way our line was brought to the crest
of the ridge above Martinpuich, and Pozieres Windmill and
the high ground north of the village were secured, and with
them observation over Martinpuich and Courcelette and the
enemy's gun positions in their neighbourhood and around
Le Sars. At a later date our troops reached the defences
of Mouquet Farm, north-west of Pozieres, and made progress
in the enemy's trenches south of Thiepval.   The enemy's
counter-attacks were incessant and frequently of great vio-
lence, but they were made in vain, and at heavy cost to him.
The fierceness of the fighting can be gathered from the fact
that one regiment of the German Guards Reserve Corps
which had been in the Thiepval salient opposite Mouquet
Farm is known to have lost 1,400 men in fifteen days.

20. The first two days of September on both Army fronts
were spent in preparation for a more general attack, which
the gradual progress made during the preceding month had
placed us in a position to undertake.   Our assault was delivered at 12 noon on the 3rd September on a front extending from our extreme right to the enemy trenches on the
right bank of the Ancre, north of Hamel. Our Allies attacked
simultaneously on our right.

Guillemont was stormed and at once consolidated, and
our troops pushed on unchecked to Ginchy and the line of
the road running south to Wedge Wood. Ginchy was also
seized, but here in the afternoon we were very strongly
counter-attacked.   For three days the tide of attack and
counter-attack swayed backwards and forwards amongst the
ruined houses of the village, till, in the end, for three days
more the greater part of it remained in the enemy's possession.   Three counter-attacks made on the evening of the

3rd September against our troops in Guillemont all failed with considerable loss to the enemy. We also gained ground north of Delville Wood and in High Wood, though here an enemy counter-attack recovered part of the ground won.

On the front of General Gough's Army, though the enemy suffered heavy losses in personnel, our gain in ground was slight.

21. In order to keep touch with the French who were attacking on our right, the assault on Falfemont Farm on the 3rd September was delivered three hours before the opening of the main assault. In the impetus of their first rush our troops reached the farm, but could not hold it. Nevertheless, they pushed on to the north of it, and on the 4th September delivered a series of fresh assaults upon it from the west and north.

Ultimately this strongly fortified position was occupied piece by piece, and by the morning of the 5th September the whole of it was in our possession. Meanwhile further progress had been made to the north-east of the farm, where considerable initiative was shown by the local commanders. By the evening of the same day our troops were established strongly in Leuze Wood, which on the following day was finally cleared of the enemy.

22. In spite of the fact that most of Ginchy and of High Wood remained in the enemy's hands, very noteworthy progress had been made in the course of these four days' operations, exceeding anything that had been achieved since the 14th July. Our right was advanced on a front of nearly two miles to an average depth of nearly one mile, penetrating the enemy's original second line of defence on this front, and capturing strongly fortified positions at Falfemont Farm, Leuze Wood, Guillemont, and south-east of Delville Wood, where we reached the western outskirts of Ginchy. More important than this gain in territory was the fact that the barrier which for seven weeks the enemy had maintained against our further advance had at last been broken. Over

1,000 prisoners were made and many machine guns taken or destroyed in the course of the fighting.

23. Preparations for a further attack upon Ginchy continued without intermission, and at 4.45 p.m. on the 9th September the attack was reopened on the whole of the Fourth Army front. At Ginchy and to the north of Leuze Wood it met with almost immediate success. On the right the enemy's line was seized over a front of more than 1,000 yards from the south-west corner of Bouleaux Wood in a north-westerly direction to a point just south of the Guillemont-Morval tramway. Our troops again forced their way into Ginchy, and passing beyond it carried the line of enemy trenches to the east. Further progress was made east of Delville Wood and south and east of High Wood.

Over 500 prisoners were taken in the operations of the 9th September and following days, making the total since the 1st July over 17,000.

24. Meanwhile the French had made great progress on our right, bringing their line forward to Leuze Wood (just south of Combles)–Le Forest–Clery-sur-Somme, all three inclusive. The weak salient in the Allied line had therefore disappeared and we had gained the front required for further operations.

Still more importance, however, lay in the proof afforded by the results described of the ability of our new Armies not only to rush the enemy's strongest defences, as had been accomplished on the 1st and 14th July, but also to wear down and break his power of resistance by a steady, relentless pressure, as they had done during the weeks of this fierce and protracted struggle. As has already been recounted, the preparations made for our assault on the 1st July had been long and elaborate; but though the enemy knew that an attack was coming, it would seem that he considered the troops already on the spot, secure in their apparently impregnable defences, would suffice to deal with it. The success of that assault, combined with the vigour and determination with which our troops pressed their advantage, and

followed by the successful night attack of the 14th July, all
served to awaken him to a fuller realisation of his danger.
The great depth of his system of fortification, to which reference has been made, gave him time to reorganise his defeated
troops, and to hurry up numerous fresh divisions and more
guns. Yet in spite of this, he was still pushed back, steadily
and continuously. Trench after trench, and strong point
after strong point, were wrested from him. The great majority of his frequent counter-attacks failed completely, with
heavy loss; while the few that achieved temporary local
success purchased it dearly, and were soon thrown back from
the ground they had for the moment regained.

The enemy had, it is true, delayed our advance considerably, but the effort had cost him dear; and the comparative collapse of his resistance during the last few days
of the struggle justified the belief that in the long run decisive victory would lie with our troops, who had displayed
such fine fighting qualities and such indomitable endurance
and resolution.

THE SITUATION IN EARLY SEPTEMBER

25. Practically the whole of the forward crest of the
main ridge, on a front of some 9,000 yards from Delville
Wood to the road above Mouquet Farm, was now in our
hands, and with it the advantage of observation over the
slopes beyond. East of Delville Wood, for a further 3,000
yards to Leuze Wood, we were firmly established on the
main ridge; while further east, across the Combles Valley,
the French were advancing victoriously on our right. But
though the centre of our line was well placed, on our flanks
there was still difficult ground to be won.

From Ginchy the crest of the high ground runs northward
for 2,000 yards, and then eastward, in a long spur, for nearly
4,000 yards. Near the eastern extremity of this spur stands
the village of Morval, commanding a wide field of view and

fire in every direction. At Leuze Wood my right was still 2,000 yards from its objective at this village, and between lay a broad and deep branch of the main Combles Valley, completely commanded by the Morval spur, and flanked, not only from its head north-east of Ginchy, but also from the high ground east of the Combles Valley, which looks directly into it.

Up this high ground beyond the Combles Valley the French were working their way towards their objective at Sailly-Saillisel, situated due east of Morval, and standing at the same level. Between these two villages the ground falls away to the head of the Combles Valley, which runs thence in a south-westerly direction. In the bottom of this valley lies the small town of Combles, then well fortified and strongly held, though dominated by my right at Leuze Wood, and by the French left on the opposite heights. It had been agreed between the French and myself that an assault on Combles would not be necessary, as the place could be rendered untenable by pressing forward along the ridges above it in on either side.

The capture of Morval from the south presented a very difficult problem, while the capture of Sailly-Saillisel, at that time some 3,000 yards to the north of the French left, was in some respects even more difficult. The line of the French advance was narrowed almost to a defile by the extensive and strongly fortified wood of St. Pierre Vaast on the one side, and on the other by the Combles Valley, which, with the branches running out from it, and the slope on each side, is completely commanded, as has been pointed out, by the heights bounding the valley on the east and west.

On my right flanks, therefore, the progress of the French and British forces was still interdependent, and the closest co-operation continued to be necessary in order to gain the further ground required to enable my centre to advance on a sufficiently wide front. To cope with such a situation unity of command is usually essential, but in this case the cordial good feeling between the Allied Armies, and the earnest desire of each to assist the other, proved equally effective, and removed all difficulties.

On my left flank the front of General Gough's Army bent back from the main ridge near Mouquet Farm down a spur descending south-westwards, and then crossed a broad valley to the Wonderwork, a strong point situated in the enemy's front-line system near the southern end of the spur on the higher slopes of which Thiepval stands. Opposite this part of our line we had still to carry the enemy's original defences on the main ridge above Thiepval, and in the village itself, defences which may fairly be described as being as nearly impregnable as nature, art, and the unstinted labour of nearly two years could make them.

Our advance on Thiepval, and on the defences above it, had been carried out up to this date, in accordance with my instructions given on the 3rd July, by a slow and methodical progression, in which great skill and much patience and endurance had been displayed with entirely satisfactory results. General Gough's Army had, in fact, acted most successfully in the required manner as a pivot to the remainder of the attack. The Thiepval defences were known to be exceptionally strong, and as immediate possession of them was not necessary to the development of my plans after the 1st July, there had been no need to incur the heavy casualties to be expected in an attempt to rush them. The time was now approaching, although it had not yet arrived, when their capture would become necessary; but from the positions we had now reached and those which we expected shortly to obtain, I had no doubt that they could be rushed when required without undue loss. An important part of the remaining positions required for my assault on them was now won by a highly successful enterprise carried out on the evening of the 14th September, by which the Wonderwork was stormed.

26. The general plan of the combined Allied attack which was opened on the 15th September was to pivot on the high ground south of the Ancre and north of the Albert-Bapaume road, while the Fourth Army devoted its whole effort to the rearmost of the enemy's original systems of defence between Morval and Le Sars. Should our success in this direction warrant it I made arrangements to enable me to extend the left of the attack to embrace the villages of Martinpuich and Courcelette. As soon as our advance on this front had reached the Morval line, the time would have arrived to bring forward my left across the Thiepval Ridge. Meanwhile on my right our Allies arranged to continue the line of advance in close co-operation with me from the Somme to the slopes above Combles; but directing their main effort northwards against the villages of Rancourt and Fregicourt, so as to complete the isolation of Combles and open the way for their attack upon Sailly-Saillisel.

27. A methodical bombardment was commenced at 6.0 a.m. on the 12th September and was continued steadily and uninterruptedly till the moment of attack.

At 6.20 a.m. on the 15th September the Infantry assault commenced, and at the same moment the bombardment became intense. Our new heavily armoured cars, known as "Tanks," now brought into action for the first time, successfully co-operated with the infantry, and coming as a surprise to the enemy rank and file gave valuable help in breaking down their resistance.

The advance met with immediate success on almost the whole of the front attacked. At 8.40 a.m. Tanks were seen to be entering Flers, followed by large numbers of troops. Fighting continued in Flers for some time, but by 10.0 a.m. our troops had reached the north side of the village, and by midday had occupied the enemy's trenches for some distance beyond. On our right our line was advanced to within as-

saulting distance of the strong line of defence running before
Morval, Les Bœufs and Gueudecourt, and on our left High
Wood was at last carried, after many hours of very severe
fighting, reflecting great credit on the attacking battalions.
Our success made it possible to carry out during the afternoon that part of the plan which provided for the capture
of Martinpuich and Courcelette, and by the end of the day
both these villages were in our hands. On the 18th September the work of this day was completed by the capture
of the Quadrilateral, an enemy stronghold which had hitherto
blocked the progress of our right towards Morval. Further
progress was also made between Flers and Martinpuich.

28. The result of the fighting of the 15th September and
following days was a gain more considerable than any which
had attended our arms in the course of a single operation
since the commencement of the offensive. In the course of
one day's fighting we had broken through two of the enemy's
main defensive systems and had advanced on a front of over
six miles to an average depth of a mile. In the course of this
advance we had taken three large villages, each powerfully
organised for prolonged resistance. Two of these villages had
been carried by assault with short preparation in the course
of a few hours' fighting. All this had been accomplished
with a small number of casualties in comparison with the
troops employed, and in spite of the fact that, as was afterwards discovered, the attack did not come as a complete surprise to the enemy.

The total number of prisoners taken by us in these operations since their commencement on the evening of the 14th
September amounted at this date to over 4,000, including
127 officers.

29. Preparations for our further advance were again
hindered by bad weather, but at 12.35 p.m. on the 25th September, after a bombardment commenced early in the morning of the 24th, a general attack by the Allies was launched
on the whole front between the Somme and Martinpuich.
The objectives on the British front included the villages of

Morval, Les Bœufs, and Gueudecourt, and a belt of country about 1,000 yards deep curving round the north of Flers to a point midway between that village and Martinpuich. By nightfall the whole of these objectives were in our hands, with the exception of the village of Gueudecourt, before which our troops met with very serious resistance from a party of the enemy in a section of his fourth main system of defence.

On our right our Allies carried the village of Rancourt, and advanced their line to the outskirts of Fregicourt, capturing that village also during the night and early morning. Combles was therefore nearly surrounded by the Allied forces, and in the early morning of the 26th September the village was occupied simultaneously by the Allied forces, the British to the north and the French to the south of the railway. The capture of Combles in this inexpensive fashion represented a not inconsiderable tactical success. Though lying in a hollow, the village was very strongly fortified, and possessed, in addition to the works which the enemy had constructed, exceptionally large cellars and galleries, at a great depth underground, sufficient to give effectual shelter to troops and material under the heaviest bombardment. Great quantities of stores and ammunition of all sorts were found in these cellars when the village was taken.

On the same day Gueudecourt was carried, after the protecting trench to the west had been captured in a somewhat interesting fashion. In the early morning a Tank started down the portion of the trench held by the enemy from the north-west, firing its machine guns and followed by bombers. The enemy could not escape, as we held the trench at the southern end. At the same time an aeroplane flew down the length of the trench, also firing a machine gun at the enemy holding it. These then waved white handkerchiefs in token of surrender, and when this was reported by the aeroplane the infantry accepted the surrender of the garrison. By 8.30 a.m. the whole trench had been cleared, great numbers of the enemy had been killed, and 8 officers and 362 other ranks made prisoners. Our total casualties amounted to five.

30. The success of the Fourth Army had now brought our advance to the stage at which I judged it advisable that Thiepval should be taken, in order to bring our left flank into line and establish it on the main ridge above that village, the possession of which would be of considerable tactical value in future operations.

Accordingly at 12.25 p.m. on the 26th September, before the enemy had been given time to recover from the blow struck by the Fourth Army, a general attack was launched against Thiepval and the Thiepval Ridge. The objective consisted of the whole of the high ground still remaining in enemy hands extending over a front of some 3,000 yards north and east of Thiepval, and including, in addition to that fortress, the Zollern Redoubt, the Stuff Redoubt, and the Schwaben Redoubt, with the connecting lines of trenches.

The attack was a brilliant success. On the right our troops reached the system of enemy trenches which formed their objectives without great difficulty. In Thiepval and the strong works to the north of it the enemy's resistance was more desperate. Three waves of our attacking troops carried the outer defences of Mouquet Farm, and, pushing on, entered Zollern Redoubt, which they stormed and consolidated. In the strong point formed by the buildings of the Farm itself, the enemy garrison, securely posted in deep cellars, held out until 6.0 p.m., when their last defences were forced by a working party of a Pioneer Battalion acting on its own initiative.

On the left of the attack fierce fighting, in which Tanks again gave valuable assistance to our troops, continued in Thiepval during that day and the following night, but by 8.30 a.m. on the 27th September the whole of the village of Thiepval was in our hands.

Some 2,300 prisoners were taken in the course of the fighting on the Thiepval Ridge on these and the subsequent days, bringing the total number of prisoners taken in the battle area in the operations of the 14th-30th September to nearly 10,000. In the same period we had captured 27 guns, over 200 machine guns, and some 40 trench mortars.

31. On the same date the south and west sides of Stuff Redoubt were carried by our troops, together with the length of trench connecting that strong point with Schwaben Redoubt to the west and also the greater part of the enemy's defensive line eastwards along the northern slopes of the ridge. Schwaben Redoubt was assaulted during the afternoon, and in spite of counter attacks, delivered by strong enemy reinforcements, we captured the whole of the southern face of the Redoubt and pushed out patrols to the northern face and towards St. Pierre Divion.

Our line was also advanced north of Courcelette, while on the Fourth Army front a further portion of the enemy's fourth system of defence north-west of Gueudecourt was carried on a front of a mile. Between these two points the enemy fell back upon his defences running in front of Eaucourt l'Abbaye and Le Sars, and on the afternoon and evening of the 27th September our troops were able to make a very considerable advance in this area without encountering serious opposition until within a few hundred yards of this line. The ground thus occupied extended to a depth of from 500 to 600 yards on a front of nearly two miles between the Bazentin-le-Petit, Ligny, Thilloy, and Albert-Bapaume roads.

Destremont Farm, south-west of Le Sars, was carried by a single company on the 29th September, and on the afternoon of the 1st October a successful attack was launched against Eaucourt l'Abbaye and the enemy defences to the east and west of it, comprising a total front of about 3,000 yards. Our artillery barrage was extremely accurate, and contributed greatly to the success of the attack. Bomb fighting continued among the buildings during the next two days, but by the evening of the 3rd October the whole of Eaucourt l'Abbaye was in our hands.

The October Fighting

32. At the end of September I had handed over Morval to the French, in order to facilitate their attacks on Sailly-Saillisel, and on the 7th October, after a postponement rendered necessary by three days' continuous rain, our Allies made a considerable advance in the direction of the latter village. On the same day the Fourth Army attacked along the whole front from Les Bœufs to Destremont Farm in support of the operations of our Allies.

The village of Le Sars was captured, together with the Quarry to the north-west, while considerable progress was made at other points along the front attacked. In particular, to the east of Gueudecourt, the enemy's trenches were carried on a breadth of some 2,000 yards, and a footing gained on the crest of the long spur which screens the defences of Le Transloy from the south-west. Nearly 1,000 prisoners were secured by the Fourth Army in the course of these operations.

33. With the exception of his positions in the neighbourhood of Sailly-Saillisel, and his scanty foothold on the northern crest of the high ground above Thiepval, the enemy had now been driven from the whole of the ridge lying between the Tortille and the Ancre.

Possession of the north-western portion of the ridge north of the latter village carried with it observation over the valley of the Ancre between Miraumont and Hamel and the spurs and valleys held by the enemy on the right bank of the river. The Germans, therefore, made desperate efforts to cling to their last remaining trenches in this area, and in the course of the three weeks following our advance made repeated counter-attacks at heavy cost in the vain hope of recovering the ground they had lost. During this period our gains in the neighbourhood of Stuff and Schwaben Redoubts were gradually increased and secured in readiness for future operations, and I was quite confident of the ability of our troops, not only to repulse the enemy's attacks, but to clear him entirely from his last positions on the ridge whenever it should suit my plans to do so. I was, therefore, well content with the situation on this flank.

Along the centre of our line from Gueudecourt to the west of Le Sars similar considerations applied. As we were already well down the forward slopes of the ridge on this front, it was for the time being inadvisable to make any serious advance. Pending developments elsewhere all that was necessary or indeed desirable was to carry on local operations to improve our positions and to keep the enemy fully employed.

On our eastern flank, on the other hand, it was important to gain ground. Here the enemy still possessed a strong system of trenches covering the villages of Le Transloy and Beaulencourt and the town of Bapaume; but, although he was digging with feverish haste, he had not yet been able to create any very formidable defences behind this line. In this direction, in fact, we had at last reached a stage at which a successful attack might reasonably be expected to yield much greater results than anything we had yet attained. The resistance of the troops opposed to us had seriously weakened in the course of our recent operations, and there was no reason to suppose that the effort required would not be within our powers.

This last completed system of defence, before Le Transloy, was flanked to the south by the enemy's positions at Sailly-Saillisel and screened to the west by the spur lying between Le Transloy and Les Bœufs. A necessary preliminary, therefore, to an assault upon it was to secure the spur and the Sailly-Saillisel heights. Possession of the high ground at this latter village would at once give a far better command over the ground to the north and north-west, secure the flank of our operations towards Le Transloy, and deprive the enemy of observation over the Allied communications in the Combles Valley. In view of the enemy's efforts to construct new systems of defence behind the Le Transloy line, it was desirable to lose no time in dealing with the situation.

Unfortunately, at this juncture, very unfavourable weather set in and continued with scarcely a break during the remainder of October and the early part of November. Poor visibility seriously interfered with the work of our artillery, and constant rain turned the mass of hastily dug trenches for which we were fighting into channels of deep mud. The country roads, broken by countless shell craters, that cross the deep stretch of ground we had lately won, rapidly became almost impassable, making the supply of food, stores and ammunition a serious problem. These conditions multiplied the difficulties of attack to such an extent that it was found impossible to exploit the situation with the rapidity necessary to enable us to reap the full benefits of the advantages we had gained.

None the less my right flank continued to assist the operations of our Allies against Saillisel, and attacks were made to this end, whenever a slight improvement in the weather made the co-operation of artillery and infantry at all possible. The delay in our advance, however, though unavoidable, had given the enemy time to reorganise and rally his troops. His resistance again became stubborn, and he seized every favourable opportunity for counter-attacks. Trenches changed hands with great frequency, the conditions of ground making it difficult to renew exhausted supplies of bombs and ammunition, or to consolidate the ground won, and so rendering it an easier matter to take a battered trench than to hold it.

34. On the 12th and 18th September further gains were made to the east of Les Bœufs-Gueudecourt line and east of Le Sars, and some hundreds of prisoners were taken. On these dates, despite all the difficulties of ground, the French first reached and then captured the villages of Sailly-Saillisel, but the moment for decisive action was rapidly passing away, while the weather showed no signs of improvement. By this time, too, the ground had already become so bad that nothing less than a prolonged period of drying weather,

which at that season of the year was most unlikely to occur, would suit our purpose.

In these circumstances, while continuing to do all that was possible to improve my position on my right flank, I determined to press on with preparations for the exploitation of the favourable local situation on my left flank. At midday on the 21st October, during a short spell of fine, cold weather, the line of Regina Trench and Stuff Trench, from the west Courcelette-Pys road westward to Schwaben Redoubt, was attacked with complete success. Assisted by an excellent artillery preparation and barrage, our infantry carried the whole of their objectives very quickly and with remarkably little loss, and our new line was firmly established in spite of the enemy's shell fire. Over 1,000 prisoners were taken in the course of the day's fighting, a figure only slightly exceeded by our casualties.

On the 23rd October, and again on the 5th November, while awaiting better weather for further operations on the Ancre, our attacks on the enemy's positions to the east of Les Bœufs and Gueudecourt were renewed, in conjunction with French operations against the Sailly-Saillisel heights and St. Pierre Vaast Wood. Considerable further progress was achieved. Our footing on the crest of the Le Transloy Spur was extended and secured, and the much contested tangle of trenches at our junction with the French left at last passed definitely into our possession. Many smaller gains were made in this neighbourhood by local assaults during these days, in spite of the difficult conditions of the ground. In particular, on the 10th November, after a day of improved weather, the portion of Regina Trench lying to the east of the Courcelette-Pys Road was carried on a front of about 1,000 yards.

Throughout these operations the enemy's counter-attacks were very numerous and determined, succeeding indeed in the evening of the 23rd October in regaining a portion of the ground east óf Le Sars taken from him by our attack on that day. On all other occasions his attacks were broken by our artillery or infantry, and the losses incurred by him in these attempts, made frequently with considerable effectives, were undoubtedly very severe.

THE FOURTH STAGE

35. On the 9th November the long continued bad weather took a turn for the better, and thereafter remained dry and cold, with frosty nights and misty mornings, for some days. Final preparations were therefore pushed on for the attack on the Ancre, though, as the ground was still very bad in places, it was necessary to limit the operations to what it would be reasonably possible to consolidate and hold under the existing conditions.

The enemy's defences in this area were already extremely formidable when they resisted our assault on the 1st July, and the succeeding period of four months had been spent in improving and adding to them in the light of the experience he had gained in the course of our attacks further south. The hamlet of St. Pierre Divion and the villages of Beaucourt-sur-Ancre and Beaumont Hamel, like the rest of the villages forming part of the enemy's original front in this district, were evidently intended by him to form a permanent line of fortifications, while he developed his offensive elsewhere. Realising that his position in them had become a dangerous one, the enemy had multiplied the number of his guns covering this part of his line, and at the end of October introduced an additional Division on his front between Grandcourt and Hebuterne.

36. At 5 a.m. on the morning of the 11th November the special bombardment preliminary to the attack was commenced. It continued with bursts of great intensity until 5.45 a.m. on the morning of the 13th November, when it developed into a very effective barrage covering the assaulting infantry.

At that hour our troops advanced on the enemy's position

through dense fog, and rapidly entered his first line trenches on almost the whole of the front attacked, from east of Schwaben Redoubt to the north of Serre. South of the Ancre, where our assault was directed northwards against the enemy's trenches on the northern slopes of the Thiepval ridge, it met with a success altogether remarkable for rapidity of execution and lightness of cost. By 7.20 a.m. our objectives east of St. Pierre Divion had been captured, and the Germans in and about that hamlet were hemmed in between our troops and the river. Many of the enemy were driven into their dug-outs and surrendered, and at 9.0 a.m. the number of prisoners was actually greater than the attacking force. St. Pierre Divion soon fell, and in this area nearly 1,400 prisoners were taken by a single division at the expense of less than 600 casualties. The rest of our forces operating south of the Ancre attained their objectives with equal completeness and success.

North of the river the struggle was more severe, but very satisfactory results were achieved. Though parties of the enemy held out for some hours during the day in strong points at various places along his first line and in Beaumont Hamel, the main attack pushed on. The troops attacking close to the right bank of the Ancre reached their second objectives to the west and north-west of Beaucourt during the morning, and held on there for the remainder of the day and night, though practically isolated from the rest of our attacking troops. Their tenacity was of the utmost value, and contributed very largely to the success of the operations.

At nightfall our troops were established on the western outskirts of Beaucourt, in touch with our forces south of the river, and held a line along the station road from the Ancre towards Beaumont Hamel, where we occupied the village. Further north the enemy's first line system for a distance of about half-a-mile beyond Beaumont Hamel was also in our hands. Still further north—opposite Serre—the ground was so heavy that it became necessary to abandon the attack at an early stage; although, despite all difficulties, our troops had in places reached the enemy's trenches in the course of their assault.

Next morning, at an early hour, the attack was renewed between Beaucourt and the top of the spur just north of Beaumont Hamel. The whole of Beaucourt was carried, and our line extended to the north-west along the Beaucourt road across the southern end of the Beaumont Hamel spur. The number of our prisoners steadily rose, and during this and the succeeding days our front was carried forward eastwards and northwards up the slopes of the Beaumont Hamel spur.

The results of this attack were very satisfactory, especially as before its completion bad weather had set in again. We had secured the command of the Ancre valley on both banks of the river at the point where it entered the enemy's lines, and, without great cost to ourselves, losses had been inflicted on the enemy which he himself admitted to be considerable. Our final total of prisoners taken in these operations, and their development during the subsequent days, exceeded 7,200, including 149 officers.

THE REST OF THE BRITISH FRONT

37. Throughout the period dealt with in this dispatch the rôle of the other armies holding our defensive line from the northern limits of the battle front to beyond Ypres was necessarily a secondary one, but their task was neither light nor unimportant. While required to give precedence in all respects to the needs of the Somme battle, they were responsible for the security of the line held by them and for keeping the enemy on their front constantly on the alert. Their rôle was a very trying one, entailing heavy work on the troops and constant vigilance on the part of Commanders and Staffs. It was carried out to my entire satisfaction, and in an unfailing spirit of unselfish and broad-minded devotion to the

general good, which is deserving of the highest commendation.

Some idea of the thoroughness with which their duties were performed can be gathered from the fact that in the period of four and a half months from the 1st July some 360 raids were carried out, in the course of which the enemy suffered many casualties and some hundreds of prisoners were taken by us. The largest of these operations was undertaken on the 19th July in the neighbourhood of Armentieres. Our troops penetrated deeply into the enemy's defences, doing much damage to his works and inflicting severe losses upon him.

THE OBJECTS ATTAINED

38. The three main objects with which we had commenced our offensive in July had already been achieved at the date when this account closes; in spite of the fact that the heavy autumn rains had prevented full advantage being taken of the favourable situation created by our advance, at a time when he had good grounds for hoping to achieve yet more important successes.

Verdun had been relieved; the main German forces had been held on the Western front; and the enemy's strength had been very considerably worn down.

Any one of these three results is in itself sufficient to justify the Somme battle. The attainment of all three of them affords ample compensation for the splendid efforts of our troops and for the sacrifices made by ourselves and our Allies. They have brought us a long step forward towards the final victory of the Allied cause.

The desperate struggle for the possession of Verdun had invested that place with a moral and political importance out of all proportion to its military value. Its fall would undoubtedly have been proclaimed as a great victory for our enemies, and would have shaken the faith of many in our ultimate success. The failure of the enemy to capture it, despite great efforts and very heavy losses, was a severe blow to his prestige, especially in view of the confidence he had openly expressed as to the results of the struggle.

Information obtained both during the progress of the Somme battle and since the suspension of active operations has fully established the effect of our offensive in keeping the enemy's main forces tied to the Western front. A movement of German troops eastward, which had commenced in June as a result of the Russian successes, continued for a short time only after the opening of the Allied attack. Thereafter the enemy forces that moved east consisted, with one exception, of divisions that had been exhausted in the Somme battle, and these troops were always replaced on the Western front by fresh divisions. In November the strength of the enemy in the Western theatre of war was greater than in July, notwithstanding the abandonment of his offensive at Verdun. It is possible that if Verdun had fallen large forces might still have been employed in an endeavour further to exploit that success. It is, however, far more probable, in view of developments in the Eastern theatre, that a considerable transfer of troops in that direction would have followed. It is therefore justifiable to conclude that the Somme offensive not only relieved Verdun, but held large forces which would otherwise have been employed against our Allies in the east.

The third great object of the Allied operations on the Somme was the wearing down of the enemy's powers of resistance. Any statement of the extent to which this has been attained must depend in some degree on estimates. There is, nevertheless, sufficient evidence to place it beyond doubt that the enemy's losses in men and material have been very considerably higher than those of the Allies, while morally the balance of advantage on our side is still greater.

During the period under review a steady deterioration took place in the moral of large numbers of the enemy's troops Many of them, it is true, fought with the greatest determination, even in the latest encounters, but the resistance of still larger numbers became latterly decidedly feebler than it had been in the earlier stages of the battle. Aided by the great depth of his defences, and by the frequent reliefs which his resources in men enabled him to effect, discipline and training held the machine together sufficiently to enable the enemy to rally and reorganise his troops after each fresh defeat. As our advance progressed four-fifths of the total number of divisions engaged on the Western front were thrown one after another into the Somme battle, some of them twice, and some three times; and towards the end of the operations, when the weather unfortunately broke, there can be no doubt that his power of resistance had been very seriously diminished.

The total number of prisoners taken by us in the Somme battle between the 1st July and the 18th November is just over 38,000, including over 800 officers. During the same period we captured 29 heavy guns, 96 field guns and field howitzers, 136 trench mortars, and 514 machine guns.

So far as these results are due to the action of the British forces, they have been attained by troops the vast majority of whom had been raised and trained during the war. Many of them, especially amongst the drafts sent to replace wastage, counted their service by months, and gained in the Somme battle their first experience of war. The conditions under which we entered the war had made this unavoidable. We were compelled either to use hastily trained and inexperienced officers and men, or else to defer the offensive until we had trained them. In this latter case we should have failed our Allies. That these troops should have accomplished so much under such conditions, and against an Army and a nation whose chief concern for so many years has been preparation for war, constitutes a feat of which the history of our nation records no equal. The difficulties and hardships cheerfully overcome, and the endurance, determination, and invincible courage shown in meeting them, can hardly be imagined by those who have not had personal experience of the battle, even though they have themselves seen something of war.

The British Achievement

The events which I have described in this Dispatch form but a bare outline of the more important occurrences. To deal in any detail even with these without touching on the smaller fights and the ceaseless work in the trenches continuing day and night for five months, is not possible here. Nor have I deemed it permissible in this Dispatch, much as I desired to do so, to particularise the units, brigades, or divisions especially connected with the different events described. It would not be possible to do so without giving useful information to the enemy. Recommendations for individual rewards have been forwarded separately, and in due course full details will be made known. Meanwhile, it must suffice to say that troops from every part of the British Isles, and from every Dominion and quarter of the Empire, whether Regulars, Territorials, or men of the New Armies, have borne a share in the Battle of the Somme. While some have been more fortunate than others in opportunities for distinction, all have done their duty nobly.

Among all the long roll of victories borne on the colours of our regiments, there has never been a higher test of the endurance and resolution of our infantry. They have shown themselves worthy of the highest traditions of our race, and of the proud records of former wars.

Against such defences as we had to assault—far more formidable in many respects than those of the most famous fortresses in history—infantry would have been powerless without thoroughly efficient artillery preparation and support. The work of our artillery was wholly admirable, though the strain on the personnel was enormous. The excellence of the results attained was the more remarkable, in view of the shortness of the training of most of the junior officers, and of the N.C.Os. and men. Despite this, they rose to a very high level of technical and tactical skill, and the combination between artillery and infantry, on which, above everything, victory depends, was an outstanding feature of the battle. Good even in July, it improved with experience, until in the latter assaults it approached perfection.

In this combination between infantry and artillery the Royal Flying Corps played a highly important part. The admirable work of this Corps has been a very satisfactory feature of the battle. Under the conditions of modern war the duties of the Air Service are many and varied. They include the regulation and control of artillery fire by indicating targets and observing and reporting the results of rounds; the taking of photographs of enemy trenches, strong points, battery positions, and of the effect of bombardments; and the observation of the movements of the enemy behind his lines.

The greatest skill and daring has been shown in the performance of all these duties, as well as in bombing expeditions. Our Air Service has also co-operated with our infantry in their assaults, signalling the position of our attacking troops and turning machine guns on to the enemy infantry and even on to his batteries in action.

Not only has the work of the Royal Flying Corps to be carried out in all weathers and under constant fire from the ground, but fighting in the air has now become a normal procedure, in order to maintain the mastery over the enemy's Air Service. In these fights the greatest skill and determination have been shown, and great success has attended the efforts of the Royal Flying Corps. I desire to point out, however, that the maintenance of mastery in the air, which is essential, entails a constant and liberal supply of the most up-to-date machines, without which even the most skilful pilots cannot succeed.

The style of warfare in which we have been engaged offered no scope for cavalry action, with the exception of the one instance already mentioned, in which a small body of cavalry gave useful assistance in the advance on High Wood.

Intimately associated with the artillery and infantry in attack and defence the work of various special services contributed much towards the successes gained.

Trench mortars, both heavy and light, have become an important adjunct to artillery in trench warfare, and valuable work has been done by the personnel in charge of these weapons. Considerable experience has been gained in their use, and they are likely to be employed even more frequently in the struggle in future.

Machine guns play a great part—almost a decisive part under some conditions—in modern war, and our Machine Gun Corps has attained to considerable proficiency in their use, handling them with great boldness and skill. The highest value of these weapons is displayed on the defensive rather than in the offensive, and we were attacking. Nevertheless, in attack also machine guns can exercise very great influence in the hands of men with a quick eye for opportunity and capable of a bold initiative. The Machine Gun Corps, though comparatively recently formed, has done very valuable work and will increase in importance.

The part played by the new armoured cars—known as "Tanks"—in some of the later fights has been brought to notice by me already in my daily reports. These cars proved of great value on various occasions, and the personnel in charge of them performed many deeds of remarkable valour.

The employment by the enemy of gas and of liquid flame as weapons of offence compelled us not only to discover ways to protect our troops from their effects but also to devise means to make use of the same instruments of destruction. Great fertility of invention has been shown, and very great credit is due to the special personnel employed for the rapidity and success with which these new arms have been developed and perfected, and for the very great devotion to duty they have displayed in a difficult and dangerous service. The Army owes its thanks to the chemists, physiologists and physicists of the highest rank who devoted their energies to enabling us to surpass the enemy in the use of a means of warfare which took the civilised world by surprise. Our own experience of the numerous experiments and trials necessary before gas and flame could be used, of the great preparations which had to be made for their manufacture, and of the special training required for the personnel employed, shows that the employment of such methods by the Germans was not the result of a desperate decision, but had been prepared for deliberately.

Since we have been compelled, in self-defence, to use similar methods, it is satisfactory to be able to record, on the evidence of prisoners, of documents captured, and of our own observation, that the enemy has suffered heavy casualties from our gas attacks, while the means of protection adopted by us have proved thoroughly effective.

Throughout the operations Engineer troops, both from home and overseas, have played an important *rôle*, and in every engagement the Field Companies, assisted by Pioneers, have co-operated with the other arms with the greatest gallantry and devotion to duty.

In addition to the demands made on the services of the Royal Engineers in the firing line, the duties of the Corps during the preparation and development of the offensive embraced the execution of a vast variety of important works, to which attention has already been drawn in this dispatch. Whether in or behind the firing line, or on the lines of communication, these skilled troops have continued to show the power of resource and the devotion to duty by which they have ever been characterised.

The Tunnelling Companies still maintain their superiority over the enemy underground, thus safeguarding their comrades in the trenches. Their skill, enterprise and courage have been remarkable, and, thanks to their efforts, the enemy has nowhere been able to achieve a success of any importance by mining.

During the Battle of the Somme the work of the Tunnelling Companies contributed in no small degree to the successful issue of several operations.

The Field Survey Companies have worked throughout with ability and devotion, and have not only maintained a constant supply of the various maps required as the battle progressed, but have in various other ways been of great assistance to the artillery.

The Signal Service, created a short time before the war began on a very small scale, has expanded in proportion with the rest of the Army, and is now a very large organisation.

It provides the means of inter-communication between all the Armies and all parts of them, and in modern war requirements in this respect are on an immense and elaborate scale. The calls on this service have been very heavy, entailing a most severe strain, often under most trying and dangerous conditions. Those calls have invariably been met with conspicuous success, and no service has shown a more whole-hearted and untiring energy in the fulfilment of its duty.

The great strain of the five months' battle was met with equal success by the Army Service Corps and the Ordnance Corps, as well as by all the other Administrative Services and Departments, both on the Lines of Communication and in front of them. The maintenance of large armies in a great battle under modern conditions is a colossal task. Though bad weather often added very considerably to the difficulties of transport, the troops never wanted for food, ammunition, or any of the other many and varied requirements for the supply of which these Services and Departments are responsible. This fact in itself is the highest testimony that can be given to the energy and efficiency with which the work was conducted.

In connection with the maintenance and supply of our troops, I desire to express the obligation of the Army to the Navy for the unfailing success with which, in the face of every difficulty, the large numbers of men and the vast quantities of material required by us have been transported across the seas.

I also desire to record the obligation of the Army in the Field to the various authorities at home, and to the workers under them—women as well as men—by whose efforts and self-sacrifice all our requirements were met. Without the vast quantities of munitions and stores of all sorts provided, and without the drafts of men sent to replace wastage, the efforts of our troops could not have been maintained.

The losses entailed by the constant fighting threw a specially heavy strain on the Medical Services. This has been met with the greatest zeal and efficiency. The gallantry and devotion with which officers and men of the regimental medical service and Field Ambulances have discharged their duties is shown by the large number of the R.A.M.C. and Medical Corps of the Dominions who have fallen in the Field. The work of the Medical Services behind the front has been no less arduous. The untiring professional zeal and marked ability of the surgical specialists and consulting surgeons, combined with the skill and devotion of the medical and nursing staffs, both at the Casualty Clearing Stations in the Field and the Stationary and General Hospitals at the Base, have been beyond praise. In this respect also the Director General has on many occasions expressed to me the immense help the British Red Cross have been to him in assisting the R.A.M.C. in their work.

The health of the troops has been most satisfactory, and, during the period to which this dispatch refers, there has been an almost complete absence of wastage due to disease of a preventable nature.

With such large forces as we now have in the Field, the control exercised by a Commander-in-Chief is necessarily restricted to a general guidance, and great responsibilities devolve on the Army Commanders.

In the Somme Battle these responsibilities were entrusted to Generals Sir Henry Rawlinson and Sir Hubert Gough, commanding respectively the Fourth and Fifth Armies, who for five months controlled the operations of very large forces in one of the greatest, if not absolutely the greatest struggle that has ever taken place.

It is impossible to speak too highly of the great qualities displayed by these commanders throughout the battle. Their thorough knowledge of the profession, and their cool and sound judgment, tact and determination proved fully equal to every call on them. They entirely justified their selection for such responsible commands.

The preparations for the battle, with the exception of those at Gommecourt, were carried out under Sir Henry Rawlinson's orders. It was not until after the assault of the 1st July that Sir Hubert Gough was placed in charge of a portion of the front of attack, in order to enable Sir Henry Rawlinson to devote his whole attention to the area in which I then decided to concentrate the main effort.

The Army Commanders have brought to my notice the excellent work done by their Staff Officers and Technical Advisers, as well as by the various commanders and staffs serving under them, and I have already submitted the names of the various officers and others recommended by them.

I desire also to record my obligation to my own Staff at General Headquarters and on the Lines of Communication, and to the various Technical Advisers attached thereto for their loyal and untiring assistance.

Throughout the operations the whole Army has worked with a remarkable absence of friction and with a self-sacrifice and whole-hearted devotion to the common cause which is beyond praise. This has ensured and will continue to ensure the utmost concentration of effort. It is indeed a privilege to work with such officers and with such men.

I cannot close this dispatch without alluding to the happy relations which continue to exist between the Allied Armies and between our troops and the civil population in France and Belgium. The unfailing co-operation of our Allies, their splendid fighting qualities, and the kindness and goodwill universally displayed towards us have won the gratitude, as well as the respect and admiration, of all ranks of the British Armies.

The Future Prospects

In conclusion, I desire to add a few words as to future prospects.

The enemy's power has not yet been broken, nor is it yet possible to form an estimate of the time the war may last before the objects for which the Allies are fighting have been attained. But the Somme battle has placed beyond doubt the ability of the Allies to gain those objects. The German Army is the mainstay of the Central Powers, and a full half of that Army, despite all the advantages of the defensive, supported by the strongest fortifications, suffered defeat on the Somme this year. Neither victors nor the vanquished will forget this; and, though bad weather has given the enemy a respite, there will undoubtedly be many thousands in his ranks who will begin the new campaign with little confidence in their ability to resist our assaults or to overcome our defence.

Our new Armies entered the battle with the determination to win and with confidence in their power to do so. They have proved to themselves, to the enemy, and to the world that this confidence was justified, and in the fierce struggle they have been through they have learned many valuable lessons which will help them in the future.

I have the honour to be,

Your Lordship's obedient Servant,

D. HAIG,

General, Commanding-in-Chief,

British Armies in France.

APPENDIX II

EXPERIENCES OF THE IV. GERMAN CORPS IN THE BATTLE OF THE SOMME DURING JULY, 1916

GENERAL SIXT VON ARMIN'S REPORT

I. ENGLISH TACTICS

1. *Infantry*

The English infantry has undoubtedly learnt much since the autumn offensive. It shows great dash in the attack, a factor to which immense confidence in its overwhelming artillery probably greatly contributes. The Englishman also has his physique and training in his favour. Commanders, however, in difficult situations, showed that they were not yet equal to their tasks. The men lost their heads and surrendered if they thought they were cut off. It was most striking how the enemy assembled and brought up large bodies of troops in close order into our zone of fire. The losses caused by our artillery fire were consequently large. One must, however, acknowledge the skill with which the English rapidly consolidate captured positions.

The English infantry showed great tenacity in defence. This was especially noticeable in the case of small parties, which, when once established with machine guns in the corner of a wood or a group of houses, were very difficult to drive out.

Generally speaking, however, our infantry returned from

the fight filled with the conviction that it was superior to the English infantry.

2. *Artillery*

Particularly noticeable was the high percentage of medium and heavy guns with the artillery, which apart from this was numerically far superior to ours. The ammunition has apparently improved considerably.

All our tactically important positions were methodically bombarded by the English artillery, as well as all known infantry and battery positions. Extremely heavy fire was continuously directed on the villages situated immediately behind the firing line, as well as on all natural cover afforded by the ground. Registration and fire control were assisted by well organised aerial observation. At night the villages also were frequently bombed by aeroplanes.

3. *Cavalry*

The frontal attacks over open ground against a portion of our unshaken infantry, carried out by several English cavalry regiments, which had to retire with heavy losses, give some indication of the tactical knowledge of the Higher Command.

II. Organisation

4. *Allotment of Special Formations for the Battle*

The reports on the experience in the Battle of the Somme, submitted to Corps H.Q., unanimously agree as to the necessity for an increased allotment of weapons, means of communication and transport of all kinds, such as, Flammenwerfer, anti-aircraft sections, anti-aircraft machine guns, captive balloons, reconnaissance and battle planes, double telephone sections, motor-lorries, horse-drawn vehicles, motor-cycles, bicycles, light-signalling detachments, wireless stations, etc. The heavy fighting has undoubtedly proved the great value and the necessity for the allotment of all these means of warfare. On the other hand, it is not considered possible to allot all these permanently to, and as part of the war establishment of, Divisions and Corps, on as large a scale as is required.

It is therefore necessary to hold ready in reserve for large operations sufficient numbers of additional units of the above mentioned description, under Army or General Headquarters, just as is done in the case of heavy artillery, battle-plane squadrons and pioneer formations, and to place them at the disposal of new Corps brought up for the battle.

In this memorandum a permanent increase of personnel and matériel has only been asked for on the scale considered necessary for the normal conditions of trench warfare.

5. *Increasing the Staffs*

The composition of the staffs of the Higher Commands, which have been reduced during the war, proved inadequate in actual fighting. It is necessary to detail to staffs, as soon as the nature of the tasks is known, a sufficient number of orderly officers, and intelligence and liaison officers. The orderly officers are at the disposal of the commander concerned, chiefly for the collection of intelligence in the front line.

6. *Corps Headquarters*

The staffs of the XIV. Reserve Corps and the IV. Corps were quartered for several days in the same building.

They had to share the available telephone communications during that time. This caused difficulties, which were particularly felt during critical periods in the fighting, when all branches of both staffs were working at extremely high pressure at the same time.

7. *Drafts in Reserve for the Infantry Companies*

In the 5th Division, a fourth platoon was formed in the infantry companies. At first, these reinforcements for replacing casualties were kept back with the 1st line transport (field kitchens). They were sent forward only when the losses of the three other platoons made reinforcements necessary. When they went forward, the fourth platoon took with it all that had been found necessary in the particular fighting (hand grenades, entrenching tools, rations, etc.). This arrangement proved very successful.

8. *Infantry Pioneer Companies*

The infantry pioneer companies of each infantry regiment of the Corps proved of great value. Full use, however, was not made of their special training, as the fighting provided them with more urgent work. These companies, which consisted of men of experience and accustomed to work together, proved most valuable in the many difficult and unexpected problems which continually faced the regiments:—for instance, in the provision of the front line trenches with the matériel necessary for carrying on the fight.

9. *Increase in Machine Guns*

A wish is generally expressed for an increase in the number of machine guns. Their value in defence has again been shown, particularly in those cases where gaps in our position, caused by a long continued, concentrated, heavy artillery fire, could not be filled.

Machine gun reserves, with the necessary men, ought undoubtedly to be provided for every Regiment, Brigade and Division. On the whole, it is considered to be very desirable to have at least 30 machine guns for every infantry regiment.

III. TRAINING

10. *Training*

The instructions based on our previous experience in defence and attack all took for granted a carefully constructed trench system. The troops on the Somme found practically no trenches at all.

The front line, and the ground for a considerable distance behind the fighting front, was kept under fire by the enemy's artillery; this fire was almost continuous and of a volume never before experienced. Several lessons for the training of the troops were learnt as the result of this bombardment; the most important ones, on which all the troops are agreed, are the following:—

> Every individual must be trained to the highest possible degree of self-reliance, so that he may know how to act during the critical periods of his own or the enemy's attacks, when he must generally be left to his own resources, and is beyond the control of his superiors.

> Crossing ground which is being heavily shelled.

> Training of the infantry in establishing relays of runners.

> Increase in the personnel trained in the use of our own and captured machine guns (officers and men).

> Training in the use of all kinds of German hand grenades.

> Training as many men as possible in the use of the enemy's hand grenades.

> Attacks by sectors, according to time table, following close up to our barrage. Formations organised in as great depth as possible to be able to cope with surprises. The absolute necessity of this has again been proved in attacking in wooded country with a restricted range of vision.

> Rapid execution of counter-attacks over open ground under different conditions. Bombers in front, skirmishers about 10 metres behind them, a number of small bodies in support slightly further in rear. In wooded country these move in file, otherwise in extended order.

> Training in the rapid preparation of shell holes

for defence, and in digging trenches by small parties in captured ground. Marching in file to form up on the tracing tape.

The employment of improvised materials in constructing defences if prepared materials are not available.

IV. Lessons from the Fighting

A. Construction of Positions and the Defence

11. *Infantry Positions*

Narrow trenches with steep sides again proved very disadvantageous and caused considerably more casualties (men being buried) than shallower trenches with a wide sole. This result is due to the fact that the splinter effect of the majority of English shells is not as good as their destructive effect. One regiment is of opinion that the garrison is better protected if the men lie down or crouch at the bottom of the trench without any further cover, than it is if the so-called "rabbit-holes" are used.

A cover trench roughly parallel to the front fire trench is not sound. Such trenches are destroyed by the enemy's fire at the same time, and in exactly the same way, as the actual fire trenches. To obviate this, trenches sited more in accordance with the ground, and consequently with certain irregularity of trace, are recommended instead of the formal type of cover trench hitherto in vogue.

The Lochmann wire entanglement ("carpet" entanglement) has not proved satisfactory, as its transport is too difficult. A better method is that of screw posts and barbed wire, which is cut up into 20-30 metre lengths under cover, and then fastened to the posts.

Curved sheet iron frames are considered a suitable substitute for timber frames, as their elasticity frequently enables them to keep out heavy shells.

12. *Artillery Positions*

The English custom of shelling villages heavily, led to the adoption of the principle that batteries should never be sited in the villages themselves, but at least 100 metres away. In this manner the casualties of the artillery were considerably diminished.

The employment of steep slopes for battery positions must also be discarded for similar reasons. When not possible to site batteries alongside existing fire trenches, etc., which are not in use, it has been found best, having regard to English methods of fighting, to select sites for batteries in open country which is merely concealed from direct observation. The main essential is, of course, that such positions in the open should be immediately concealed from aeroplane observation. Wire netting, tent squares, etc., covered with material found on the surface of the ground round the position, have proved useful. As material for the construction of dug-outs arrived, a greater degree of security was attained.

13. *Battle Headquarters*

Battle Headquarters, also, when the artillery fire is so heavy, should not be sited in villages, on steep slopes, or at other points which stand out conspicuously on the ground or on the map. In cases where the existing telephone system necessitated the utilisation of such unsuitable points as Battle Headquarters, it resulted in frequent interruptions in personal and telephone traffic by artillery fire, and overcrowding in the few available cellars in the villages.

Staffs when going into their Battle Headquarters must see that there are as many clear signboards as possible to indicate the way to them. Owing to lengthy searches for Battle Headquarters, many casualties have occurred which might have been avoided.

14. *Relief of Infantry and Pioneers*

When troops are relieved in the trenches, it is of the utmost importance that the outgoing troops are careful in handing over the position. Whenever the tactical conditions permit, this should take place on the spot, the various commanders and subordinate commanders meeting together for the purpose. At any rate, it is absolutely essential that the incoming troops should be thoroughly informed as to the tactical situation, by means of personal conferences between the outgoing and incoming commanders, with the assistance of maps and sketches which will be taken over by the latter. A perfectly clear picture must be given of the state of the positions, etc., particularly of their weak points, and also of any work which it had been intended to carry out, the degree of importance attached to it being specified.

In order that a relief may be properly carried out, it is also necessary that the commanders of the incoming troops should acquaint themselves, by daylight, with the lie of the ground; it may be necessary to send them on ahead in motor cars. The troops, too, must if possible be able to gain a general idea of the position while it is still daylight. Reliefs must therefore, unless there are cogent reasons against it, be begun at dusk and completed during the early hours of the night.

If it is impossible to give the incoming troops an idea of the ground beforehand, then detachments of the outgoing troops must be left behind in the trenches. It is very important that the junction points with other troops should be absolutely clearly indicated, as these are so easily forgotten when reliefs are carried out under heavy fire.

Losses on the march up to the trenches can be minimized if the stretches of ground which are under fire are crossed in as small parties as possible. One Infantry Brigade recommends that the relief be carried out by platoons, at short intervals of time, and considers that the troops should move up in file. No hard and fast rules can be laid down. The choice of the formation in which the troops are to move will always depend on the nature of the ground.

When troops which are advancing are to be relieved, as much engineering and constructional material as possible must be taken with the relieving troops. In all cases the men must carry as many large entrenching tools as they can.

15. *Engagement and Relief of Artillery*

The same principles hold good for the relief of batteries as for infantry. If the tactical situation is such that reinforcing batteries have to be brought up at night, without having had time to reconnoitre by day, then the want of knowledge of the ground must at least be counterbalanced by getting into touch as soon as possible with the artillery already in position, and by making the fullest possible use of the knowledge of the ground which that artillery possesses. If the reinforcements come under the orders of Artillery Commanders who are already in command in the sector, the staffs and officers already engaged must, as soon as it is known that reinforcing batteries are to be brought up, be detailed to reconnoitre battery positions for the commanders who have not yet arrived. The officers who carry out these reconnaissances must then be allotted as guides to the new batteries when these move up into position.

16. *Distribution of the Infantry*

One of the most important lessons drawn from the Battle of the Somme is that, under heavy, methodical artillery fire, the front line should be only thinly held, but by reliable men and a few machine guns, even when there is always a possibility of a hostile attack. When this was not done, the casualties were so great before the enemy's attack was launched, that the possibility of the front line repulsing the attack by its own unaided efforts was very doubtful. The danger of the front line being rushed when so lightly held must be overcome by placing supports (infantry and machine guns), distributed in groups according to the ground, as close as possible behind the foremost fighting line. Their task is to rush forward to reinforce the front line at the moment the enemy attacks, without waiting for orders from the rear. In all cases where this procedure was adopted, we succeeded in repulsing and inflicting very heavy losses on the enemy, who imagined that he had merely to drop into a trench filled with dead.

The essential conditions for success are, therefore, that the various formations should be organised in depth but that their units should be employed side by side. Only in this way is it possible to ensure that a counter-attack in sufficient strength and with unmixed units can be made, if the enemy has succeeded in penetrating the line, an occurrence which cannot always be avoided when the artillery fire is so heavy.

Even the Company Commander must, in no circumstances, neglect to provide himself with a reserve consisting of a few groups and, if possible, of machine guns as well. The Sub-sector Commanders must also have at all times sufficient troops at their disposal to be able at once to drive the enemy out, by means of a counter-attack, should he succeed in pene-trating into the position. It is self-evident that Regimental and Higher Commanders must have complete units at their disposal as a reserve. The more troops that are held in reserve the better. A considerably greater allotment of machine guns by Army Headquarters when troops are moved to the battle front is absolutely necessary, as this will enable infantry to be held in reserve on a sufficiently large scale. The great advantage offered by the increased possi-bility of exchanging the garrison of the front line with the reserves, is perfectly obvious.

17. *Organisation of the Artillery*

The formation of Corps Artillery was ordered by Army Headquarters with the object of avoiding, at any rate as far as the more permanent heavy artillery was concerned, the frequent changes in command, due to the frequent changes of the Field Artillery Brigades. From the experience now gained, it seems advisable to place a few heavy batteries under the Commanders of the Divisional Artillery, in order to enable them to carry out all the tasks allotted to them as rapidly as possible.

18. *Reserve of Personnel and Matériel for the Artillery*

The supply of fresh guns was usually carried out rapidly. Nevertheless, it is very desirable that each Field Artillery Brigade should retain a few guns, with their detachments, to act as a reserve. Possibly it might be sound only to engage two of the three batteries of an *Abteilung* at first, and to retain one in reserve to replace casualties. Heavy batteries of four guns should only have three of their guns in position during such critical fighting, in order to have a reserve available for immediate use.

19. *Artillery Barrage Fire*

It was found very difficult to form a continuous barrage, without gaps, in front of our own lines, owing to the occasional uncertainty as to the position of our front line, which was continually changing during the fighting, the frequent changing of batteries, the re-grouping of the artillery which was often necessary, the bad conditions for observation, the permanent interruption of the telephone communications, and the practically continuous heavy fire which was maintained behind our front line.

Whenever we were successful in establishing such a barrage in a comparatively short time, it was entirely due to the forward artillery observation officers. The only means of communication which these officers possessed, as a rule, were light-pistols and runners. By full use of these means it was possible to carry out an approximate registration. The method employed was for the battery, at the exact time previously agreed upon, to open fire with a definite number of rounds on a point which was easy to observe. The fall of the shell relative to this point served as the basis of the registration for the barrage in front of a specified sector. It was necessary to supplement these observations by means of personal verbal reports. It was found specially useful for artillery observation officers, who relieved each other, to go forward twice a day. This, unfortunately, led to heavy casualties among artillery officers, but saved the infantry many losses. (Regarding the action of the artillery observation officers during an attack, *see* para. IV. C. 34.)

In cases where it was not possible to register for the barrage in the ordinary manner, the employment of various natures of shell (time shrapnel, time H.E. shell and percussion H.E. shell), fired at various ranges, proved to be a useful expedient for a barrage. The different effects of the various natures of shell at any rate caused the fire to be distributed in depth and breadth over a considerable area. The disadvantage of this method is the large expenditure of ammunition incurred, without which the desired effect cannot be obtained.

20. *Barrage Fire of Infantry and Snipers*

Over ground which cannot be observed, and at night, the unaimed but horizontal barrage fire of infantry and machine guns, during and immediately after critical periods, affords rest and protection to troops who are probably shaken for the moment, and not only scares the enemy but inflicts losses on him.

The excellent results obtained from selected snipers posted at good view points, in trees, etc., are particularly emphasised by one Regiment.

21. *Action to Be Taken During Continuous Heavy Shelling*

It has been found to be a good plan, during the continuous heavy bombardment of incomplete front line positions, for the garrison to advance 100-200 metres and to lie down in the open without any cover.

It is advisable for a battery, the position of which has been discovered by the enemy, not to change its position in such circumstances, but to increase its cover as much as possible, as every new battery position is soon discovered when the enemy's aerial activity is so great. Further, frequent changes of position, involving new digging-in and the removal of the ammunition during the same night if possible, are beyond the strength of the detachments, which has already been taxed by continuous firing.

22. Employment of "Green Cross" (Gas) Shell

The wish expressed in many quarters that the question of firing with "green cross" (gas) shell should be left to the Artillery Commanders of Divisions, with a view to taking better advantage of the tactical situation, could not be acceded to, as the employment of this ammunition depends too much on the nature of the ground and weather conditions, which can only be fully appreciated by experts, and these were all, in the case in question, at the Army Group Headquarters.

It is, however, sound, if sufficient field artillery is available, to allot permanently several batteries for the purpose of firing with "green cross" ammunition so as to avoid taking away batteries for firing with it from the Divisional Artillery Commanders without previous notice, at a time when their services are being relied on for the execution of other tasks. During the periods when it is not possible to fire with "green cross" ammunition (for instance, almost always during the day time), the batteries will be at the disposal of Artillery Commanders as reinforcements.

According to apparently reliable information, the effect of the "green cross" ammunition was good.

23. *Bomb-Throwers and Trench Mortars*

The "Priester" bomb-thrower again proved itself to be a very effective weapon in the fighting on the Somme.

Trench mortars, at least the light pattern, should be brought up into position at the earliest possible moment, even if the trenches are bad or if there are no trenches at all. They must not be held in reserve for fear of possible losses.

24. *Strong Points*

The preparation, for subsequent defence, of villages and other strong points afforded by the form of the ground behind the front line, cannot be begun too soon. Villages should be divided into sectors for purposes of defence, and should be provided with garrisons, however small these may be, and machine guns. Supports and reserves must not be quartered in the villages close to the line, owing to the particularly heavy shelling to which these are exposed. The boundary of a sector should never run through a village.

25. *Retired Infantry Positions and Switch Lines*

The first necessities for retired positions and the extremely important diagonal switch lines, are entanglements, dug-outs and communication trenches. The number of these positions should be increased by continual work, and by making the fullest possible use of all available forces. It is always possible to dispense with digging the fire trench, which can be comparatively quickly constructed. This point must also be kept in mind from the start, when constructing retired positions in quiet sectors.

In view of the experience gained, the following scheme appears to provide the most practical organisation for the construction of retired positions and communication trenches while fighting is in progress :—

In the front-line area (the rearward limits of which vary according to the circumstances) the work will be done by the Divisions. A responsible commander and a party of pioneers, who do not change when the Division is relieved, will be allotted to each of these positions, etc., to assist the Divisions. The working parties detailed by the Divisions will be under the command of officers from those Divisions, who are responsible for the quantity of work that is done. Particular conditions may make it necessary to attach working parties to the Divisions to prepare positions, the rapid construction of which is of great importance. These must be detailed from troops not intended to take part in the fighting, otherwise they must be provided from the Divisional reserves. It is an established principle that any detachment of troops which is holding a position in the rear must work at strengthening it.

The supervision of the Labour formations working at night requires much personnel. It is better to avoid the use of labour formations in the construction of positions which, though only occasionally, are under heavy fire.

Special officers must be detailed for the construction of positions, etc., required in the area behind the lines. These will be immediately under the orders of the Army Group or of Army Headquarters. In order to furnish the necessary labour, pioneer and labour companies must be permanently allotted to them, as well as reliefs of other available troops and the necessary transport for bringing up materials.

26. Retired Artillery Positions

Experience has shown that the important point in the construction of artillery positions behind the lines is to begin with the construction of observation posts, cable trenches, and communication trenches. Battery positions can be constructed by a battery in one night if necessary, provided that the materials are available.

27. *Method of Attack and Time Required*

Insufficiently prepared attacks and counter-attacks nearly always fail through being too hurried.

The greatest care must be taken to differentiate between counter-attacks which are undertaken immediately after the loss of a length of trench, or of any other section of ground, with reserves which are on the spot, and those which are ordered by a Higher Commander and for which the reserves of a higher formation must be brought up.

In the latter case, the full time necessary for the preparation of the attack and the disposition of troops in the front line is frequently not sufficiently considered. In this respect, it is to be noted that the transmission of orders to the front line occupies more time than is often supposed; the telephone lines are destroyed, and messengers can only work their way slowly through the enemy's barrage. Even if the order has reached the front line, it requires some time to circulate it and explain the method of carrying out the attack and its objective, to the troops, distributed, as they are, in groups. Similar difficulties arise in the case of reserves which have been brought up. They advance slowly across country with which they are generally unacquainted, and which lies under heavy fire. The commanders of the reserves have to form an idea of the tactical situation, and for this purpose are obliged to get into communication with commanders already in the front line. This all requires time and creates friction, both of which are increased at night and in country where the view is restricted (village or wood).

In the case of counter-attacks which are to be carried out with the aid of strong reserves, a thorough artillery preparation is necessary. This, too, requires time. The experience of the Battle of the Somme has again and fully confirmed the long established principle:—

A counter-attack must either follow immediately and the

decision to counter-attack must come from the front line and the forces for it must be ready to hand before the enemy's attack is entirely finished, or the counter-attack must be methodically and thoroughly prepared by the artillery and carried out with reserves who have been instructed as to the tactical situation and the nature of the ground.

If counter-attacks which, on account of the situation, ought to be methodically prepared are hurried, they cost much blood and cause the troops to lose their trust in their leaders if they fail, which nearly always happens in such a case.

28. *Approach March and Deployment*

Before bringing up troops into the zone of the enemy's artillery fire, the commander must obtain a clear idea, by means of clever scouts and by his own observation, how the enemy's fire is distributed over the ground to be crossed. When selecting the route, areas which are hardly or not under fire will be taken into consideration rather than the nature of the ground and the cultivation. Depressions and sunken roads which are invisible to the enemy are, as a rule, under such heavy barrage fire that it is not advisable to make use of them. Villages which lie in the enemy's zone of fire are to be avoided on principle.

29. *Methodical Attack*

An advance to the assault with a simultaneous lifting of our own artillery fire has proved extremely successful in attack. This was also the case when a definite rate of advance for the infantry was settled and our artillery fire was lifted step by step, in accordance with this, on a pre-arranged time table. Only in cases where the infantry, through lack of practice in this new method of attack, pushed right through was the progress of the attack checked.

30. *Assaulting Parties*

The detailing of assaulting parties in an attack has proved very useful. Their chief advantage lay in the freshness of the specially selected personnel who had not been engaged in previous fighting. The careful training beforehand of the assaulting parties resulted in these troops proving themselves quite equal to all tasks which fell to their lot in village or wood fighting. They felt that they were a body of élite troops, which indeed they proved themselves to be.

31. *Attacks in Woods*

When attacking in a wood, it is preferable, instead of the usual skirmish lines, following one after the other, to employ small assaulting columns following a single line of assault.

The empoyment of small Flammenwerfer in wooded country which is full of obstacles, and in which there is no extended view, suffers, in an attack with a distant objective, under the disadvantage of the heavy weight of the apparatus. It is better to use the Flammenwerfer from a well prepared assaulting position and against well defined, close objectives which have been previously reconnoitred.

The "Priester" bomb-throwers have been successfully used to clear out shell-holes which could not be reached with hand grenades.

32. *Procedure after a Successful Attack*

In order to be able to entrench rapidly and hold captured ground, carrying and working parties (*see* also para. XI., 65) must follow the assaulting troops under the leadership of energetic officers.

C. CO-OPERATION OF INFANTRY AND ARTILLERY

33. *Communication between Commanders*

When the Corps was put into battle, the units of the troops already engaged were very much mixed. The arrangements for artillery command were not sufficiently clear in all cases.

The bringing up of new Divisions had, on account of the tactical situation, to take place as quickly as possible and in the dark. Necessary reliefs and movements of troops were taking place almost daily.

Owing to all these circumstances and to faulty telephone communications, it was very difficult to establish touch between infantry and artillery. In many places it was a long time before touch was obtained, greatly to the disadvantage of our infantry, which was heavily engaged. The greater the difficulties in establishing this absolutely necessary touch between infantry and artillery, the greater must be the efforts of both sides to secure communication. The best means to this end is for the infantry Regimental Commander and the Artillery Group Commander to be near each other. If this is impossible, their posts must be connected by telephone as soon as possible, in order that there may be continuous change of important information. One artillery liaison officer of each of the groups in question (in certain circumstances, several groups) must remain continuously with the Infantry Regimental Commander.

34. *Communications in the Front Line*

The number and position of artillery observation officers (*see* also para. IV. A. 19) depend on the tactical situation and the ground. They must be connected with the sub-sector (battalion) Commanders in front of whose sector their artillery is working, in order to be able to receive and forward rapidly all requests and messages which come from the front line. In an attack, artillery observation officers must be sufficiently far forward to be able to observe our own front line continuously. It is not usually sound for them to remain in the foremost firing line. In country with a restricted view, as was the case in Delville Wood and Longueval village, our own front line could only be seen by the artillery observation officers if they followed immediately behind the foremost line. There still remain, of course, the difficulties of sending back important messages *as rapidly as possible*, especially those with reference to shells which fall short and so endanger our own infantry. These difficulties can be overcome by means of signals with light-pistols and by orderlies (relays), if proper arrangements are previously made, and the most reliable officers and orderlies (cyclists) are detailed for the responsible task of artillery observation and for the delivery of messages during an attack.

It may, nevertheless, happen that events on the battlefield, especially if the fire is as heavy as that in Delville Wood and Longueval, may prevent important messages from the artillery observers from reaching the fire commander sufficiently quickly. One Regiment, therefore, has made the very valuable suggestion that artillery information centres should be pushed forward as an additional safeguard. Battalions and companies should be informed of the position of these centres, so that the result of their observation and their requests can be sent there as well as to the normal centres.

V. Means of Communication

35. *Telephone Communications*

The existing telephone system proved totally inadequate in consequence of the development which the fighting took. This was aggravated by the division of the sector hitherto held by Stein's Army Group into two separate Army Groups, which required the provision of several new lines. The conditions here were, therefore, particularly unfavourable. But in trench warfare difficult conditions must always be reckoned with in this relation. It is therefore considered necessary to allot a double telephone section to each Division to reinforce the Corps Telephone Detachment, and to extend the existing lines by means of the stores in reserve, as soon as the Division arrives in the front line. The shortage of lines which was discovered to exist reacted most disadvantageously on the communication between the infantry and the artillery, and could only be by degrees made good.

It is advisable as far as possible to avoid erecting lines through villages, as they are subject to a heavy fire there. If lines start from villages, they should be diverted by the shortest route over open fields in the desired direction.

To enable lines, which have been damaged by shell fire, to be repaired as quickly as possible, it has been found useful in practice to establish permanent telephone parties in dug-outs along the lines; it is the duty of these parties to test the lines frequently and see that they are in working order.

It is most desirable that the staffs of every field artillery regiment and *Abteilung,* as well as those of every foot artillery regiment and foot artillery battalion, should be permanently provided with the larger pattern folding telephone box, so as to avoid the large number of separate boxes otherwise necessary at a regimental, or *Abteilung,* or battalion command post. These take up room and are difficult to supervise properly.

The usual practice of changing telephone apparatus when reliefs were carried out, proved to be a source of very marked interruption. It must not take place when the fighting is so severe. The outgoing units should hand over their apparatus to the units which are relieving them. These remarks apply particularly to folding telephone boxes, the removal of which caused considerable interruption in the service.

36. *Wireless Communications*

It is desirable that light wireless stations should be allotted to the staffs of infantry regiments and battalions, in order to improve the communications in the front area. They could be formed from the stores in reserve.

37. *Runners*

Runners, and the establishment of relays of runners, have proved very useful everywhere. The casualties were comparatively slight. All important information and orders should always be sent in duplicate. One Infantry Brigade recommends that 100 metres should be the normal distance between the relay stations of runners in the fire zone.

38.   *Motor-Cycles and Bicycles*

The Headquarters of Corps, Divisions, and Brigades must each have two motor-cycles from the reserve stores placed at their disposal when they go into the front line. The establishment of motor-cycles proved insufficient for the heavy fighting; this deficiency was painfully evident. The establishment of ordinary bicycles was also not sufficient for the work to be done.

39.   *Light-Signalling Lines*

The existing organisation of the light-signalling service does not meet requirements. It is considered urgently necessary that a complete light-signal detachment should be formed in each Corps. A total of about 30 signal lamps of medium range is required to enable a signal line to be established for every infantry regiment and every artillery group. Besides these, four light-signal sections, with apparatus of a greater range, are required to establish long distance light-signal communications in the Divisional sectors. The temporary allotment of light-signalling apparatus from reserve stores cannot be considered satisfactory, as the full utilisation of this method of communication depends mostly on the signal stations working well together and with their respective command posts.

Until this urgent demand can be complied with, it is suggested that an auxiliary light-signal detachment should be formed in each Division by making use of the personnel of the search-light sections. It was not possible to employ the search-light sections for their proper work in the fighting on the Somme. Good results were obtained by an attached Division, which had already formed an auxiliary light-signal detachment. Another Division of the Corps succeeded in forming two auxiliary light-signal stations, and in maintaining satisfactory communication over a distance of 12 kilometres by flashes on the horizon, although direct vision was not obtainable. The great value of communication by light-signalling was made doubly clear by the continual interruptions of the telephone communications.

40. *Light-Pistol Signals*

The communication between the front line and the artillery for the direction of barrage fire was entirely confined to light-pistol signals. It was found that three light-pistols per company are not enough, and that the ammunition supply is too small. It is considered necessary that the establishment of light-pistols should be at least doubled by additional pistols from the reserve stocks, and that a large supply of ammunition should be provided before units go into the front line. As a result of the difficulties experienced, Corps Headquarters were obliged, when the IV. Corps was relieved, to order all light-pistols the which were still available, together with their ammunition, to be handed over to its successors, although the light-pistols were part of the war establishment.

41. *Balloon and Aeroplane Observation*

The means for providing the artillery with aerial observation has proved to be insufficient. It has again been shown, as indeed had already been recognised under less difficult conditions, that it would be a great advantage to add a captive balloon and at least two observation aeroplanes to the war establishment of each Field Artillery *Brigade* (of two regiments).

Matters would not be improved by temporarily allotting these important means of obtaining observation, for good results can only be attained by continual co-operation between the observer and the fire commander.

The numerical superiority of the enemy's airmen and the fact that their machines were better, were made disagreeably apparent to us, particularly in their direction of the enemy's artillery fire and in bomb-dropping.

The English aeroplane observers also made use of sound signals to communicate with their batteries while in the air. It is very likely possible that a rapid means of communication with the batteries can be established in this way; it might be very serviceable as a complement to wireless messages, which are frequently interrupted. Experiments in this direction are being carried out in the IV, Corps.

42. *Anti-Aircraft Measures*

The number of our battle-planes was also too small. The enemy's airmen were often able to fire successfully on our troops with machine guns, by descending to a height of a few hundred metres. The German anti-aircraft gun sections could not continue firing at that height without exposing their own troops to serious danger from fragments of shell. This has produced a desire for the anti-aircraft defences to be supplemented by machine guns; these must, if necessary, be supplied from the reserve stocks. A further lesson to be learnt from this surprisingly bold procedure on the part of the English airmen, is that the infantry make too little use of their rifles as a means of driving off aircraft.

The best defensive weapons among the anti-aircraft guns were the batteries of four 10-cm. guns of the foot artillery. The anti-aircraft guns mounted on motor-cars are considered less useful for the present conditions of fighting than the stationary guns, as they continually require new telephone connections with the anti-aircraft telephone exchange system as they alter their positions.

It has already been found necessary, even in quiet sectors, to fit up some field gun sections as auxiliary anti-aircraft defences, to supplement the regular anti-aircraft gun sections.

This was still more necessary in the Battle of the Somme. It is desirable that at least one battery of each Field Artillery *Brigade* should be equipped with guns mounted on light field howitzer carriages, so as to have guns at hand which can be quickly employed either for anti-aircraft purposes or for forming a barrage. To make these guns still more useful for defence against aircraft, it is also desirable that each Field Artillery *Brigade* be equipped with portable anti-aircraft mountings (pivots) for two anti-aircraft gun sections. It would be possible to arrange for the transport of these mountings by the light ammunition column, on two-wheeled trailers.

43. *Special Reporting Detachments*

In consequence of the comparative slowness with which reports from the front line trenches reach the Higher Commanders when sent by the usual channels, it has been found necessary for commanders to make arrangements independent of these channels, and to keep themselves informed by their own agents of the course of the fighting. For this purpose the most practical method is the employment of so-called "spy-troops" (*Späh-Trupps*) as well as the orderly officers who go forward from time to time. These special reporting detachments consist of one officer and a few picked non-commissioned officers and men, equipped with infantry telephone apparatus, to connect up with existing lines. They should choose their own position, so that they can observe any particular sector in which fighting is taking place.

Their duty is to ensure that reports on the progress of the fighting reach the commander by whom they have been sent out, as quickly as possible, by means of a combined system of telephones and runners. To enable these detachments to work successfully in action, they should be formed in the Divisions during quiet periods, and be thoroughly trained in the duties which they have to perform.

VI. Arms

44. Small-Arms

Numerous complaints have been received of rifle breech-actions being completely clogged with dirt both in attack and defence. It is, therefore, advisable to fit a cover over the breech of the rifles, like that used in the English Army, which can be easily unfastened and then hangs from the rifle.

The 1908 pattern pistol has proved to be a very useful weapon for hand-to-hand fighting in villages and woods. It is also recommended by several units as a useful weapon for machine gun detachments in close fighting. One Field Artillery Regiment recommends the adoption of the new pattern sword bayonet with saw-edge, which has already been experimentally adopted for mounted troops. Automatic rifles (*Musketen*) are stated to be useful weapons for trench warfare.

45. Machine Guns

Machine guns usually have to be brought up over open ground under a heavy barrage. The great weight of the gun has again proved to be a serious disadvantage under these conditions. Even if the gun is dismounted, it is very difficult to drag up the heavy sledge over ground which is under fire. All regiments are unanimous in recommending the introduction of a lighter form of gun-carriage, modelled on that of the improvised gun-carriage used by the machine gun marksman sections. One regiment has obtained good results with a gun-carriage of its own invention, which is even lighter.

Complaints have also been received that the ammunition boxes and water-jackets of the machine guns are too heavy. It is proposed that the lighter boxes and jackets used by the machine gun marksman sections should be generally adopted.

The wheels of the machine gun hand carriages, used by the marksman sections, are not strong enough for paved roads, so that these carriages are not adapted for use on the march, but they have proved suitable for bringing the machine guns into action, and very useful for the transport of ammunition, rations and wounded.

Spare parts for machine guns must be kept in readiness in large quantities behind the front line, so that they can be brought up to the troops quickly if required.

46. Hand Grenades

The hand grenade was the most important infantry weapon both in attack and defence. It is universally suggested that the supply of hand grenades should be increased. If it is possible to ensure a supply of different kinds of hand grenades, the general opinion is in favour of the use of "Ball" and "Egg" grenades for attack, despite their small effect, in preference to cylindrical grenades with handles, as a larger supply of the two former can be taken into action.

It would appear advisable to use only one kind of hand grenade. This would simplify training in the use of hand grenades. In fighting such as we have had on the Somme, defence and attack continually alternate. It is not always possible to bring up sufficient quantities of the particular hand grenade which is best suited to the conditions of the fighting at the moment, but as the cylindrical grenade with handle is on the whole the most effective, it is recommended that this pattern should be universally adopted.

47. Guns

The guns of the field artillery proved on the whole to be thoroughly satisfactory. Their failure was usually due to the ammunition, or to the fact that the number of rounds fired was greater than the life of a tube permits. Jams were frequently experienced with field guns. These were due to steel cartridge cases (manufacturer's mark A.E.G.) and brass cartridge cases with steel base (Sp:61). These cartridges often jammed when the breech was opened, and could only be removed by the use of the rammer. The rate of fire was in consequence considerably reduced. Repeated forcible opening also damages the breech. It is true that many jams may have been due to the fact that the necessary care in the storing and handling of ammunition could not be observed under the conditions which existed on the Somme.

The buffer proved to be the weakest point of the howitzer. The leather washers burn through and the glycerine runs out. The bad working of the buffer affects the sides of the carriage, which are rather weak, so that damage easily occurs.

VII. Ammunition

48. *Various Kinds of Ammunition*

A supply of good ammunition of even quality and character is an absolute necessity for rapid preparation for action, a high rate of fire and accurate shooting, particularly if a barrage is to be placed close in front of our infantry.

The long shell of the light field howitzer was supplied with five different fuses, of which two kinds had to be fired with safety precautions. Fresh registration or ranging is required when a change is made from one ammunition to another. At critical moments, or in the dark, it is not possible to ascertain with what kind of fuse every shell is fitted. This ammunition besides is supplied without shell baskets. It is therefore difficult, and takes time, to bring the reserves of long shell up to the guns.

The old pattern of field gun ammunition has proved efficient.

The use of the "green cross" ammunition is very hard on the guns, for in consequence of the limited possibilities of using it, a great quantity of ammunition has to be expended in a short time. For example, a light field howitzer battery fired over 3,500 rounds of this ammunition in 24 hours.

49. *Expenditure of Ammunition*

The average daily expenditure of ammunition per gun during the whole period of the fighting was:—

Field guns	145 rounds
Light field howitzers	170 "
Heavy field howitzers	119 "
10-cm. guns	118 "
(21-cm.) mortars	51 "

The small expenditure of (field) gun ammunition is to be attributed to the small supplies available. Instructions had to be issued to the troops to be economical with (field) gun shell.

The highest daily average expenditure per gun reached during the period of fighting in the Army Group for the different kinds of guns was:—

Field guns	322 rounds
Light field howitzers	479 "
Heavy field howitzers	233 "
10-cm. guns	321 "
(21-cm.) mortars	116 "

The following quantity of ammunition is considered necessary:—

Battery.	In the Battery position.	In reserve with the Division.	In reserve with the Corps.
Field guns..................	2200 rounds.	500 rounds.	2200 rounds.
Light field howitzers........	2200 "	500 "	2200 "
Heavy field howitzers.......	1400 "	300 "	1400 "
10-cm. guns	1600 "	400 "	1600 "
(21-cm.) mortars (2 mortars).	300 "	80 "	300 "

Large quantities of ammunition can only be provided near the battery by extensive distribution in the surrounding country. Carrying ammunition over long distances by men must be avoided, as their endurance is fully taxed day and night by firing and entrenching. The more ammunition is collected near the battery position, the more will be exploded by being hit. Another result of storing large quantities of ammunition in the battery position is that, on changing position, a large part of it must be left behind in the old position, the subsequent removal of which, if indeed this is possible, can only be accomplished with the greatest difficulty.

50. *Ammunition Supply*

The supply of artillery ammunition of all kinds, during the first days of the battle, did not equal the great expenditure. Reserve supplies were only available in very small quantities. On the 14th July an English attack took place, which necessitated a great expenditure of ammunition. It was impossible to replenish the supply in the battery positions from the ammunition brought up by the L. of C., or from the ammunition depots of the Army Groups, to such an extent as to ensure that the requirements for the next day would be met. The Army Group was compelled to ask for ammunition from Stein's Army Group, and this had to be partly brought up by night, under difficult conditions, from the advanced ammunition depots of the two Divisions nearest to the Army Group in the North.

From the 15th July onwards, the supply of ammunition was better. The amount sent up to the batteries was made up by supplies from the L. of C. in such quantities that, as a general rule, the amount of ammunition laid down in para. 49, as being necessary in the battery positions and in reserve with the Divisions, was always available. The Army Group was also able to collect gradually a small reserve of ammunition (exclusively field-gun ammunition), but the supply was never sufficient to make good the expenditure in the event of the railway being blocked for one or two days. The lack of gun ammunition was always felt, and large reserves were never available. It is true that Army Headquarters always succeeded in bringing up the gun ammunition trains quickly, and sending the ammunition from these trains to the battery positions, but a block on the railway might have had serious consequences. It is absolutely necessary to place so much ammunition at the disposal of the Army Groups that the above mentioned "iron rations" are available in the battery positions, and in the Divisional and Corps ammunition depots.

The supply of ammunition was arranged for by Corps Headquarters as far as the Corps and Divisional depots. Motor-lorries, artillery ammunition columns, and infantry ammunition columns, supply parks and supply columns equipped with heavy country carts, were all under one organisation. As soon as the arrival of the trains was announced, the columns were despatched to the detraining stations. The means of transport were sufficient. The Divisions had at their disposal the battery and light ammunition columns, one supply park or supply column, and in some cases a foot artillery ammunition column as well.

Motor-lorry columns have been very efficient, and have carried out their duties very satisfactorily. The allotment of the country carts to the columns which were used as a temporary measure to bring up artillery ammunition, proved a practical arrangement.

There should be ammunition depots for a large quantity of ammunition close to the detraining stations. In addition, light railways are required from the detraining stations to the depots. These were not provided, and consequently a large quantity of ammunition was piled up along the railway lines immediately beside the detraining station.

VIII. ENGINEER STORES

51. *Pioneer Park Detachment*

A pioneer park detachment must be available in every Corps to take over the management of the parks and the supply of engineer stores, as soon as the Corps is moved into a new position. Until an establishment for it is approved, the detachment must consist of troops drawn from the Corps, but it must be formed before the Corps takes up its new position. The Pioneer Commander must have a suitable officer at his disposal, who will be in charge of the supply of stores; he should not, if possible, be on the establishment of any pioneer unit. The park detachment must be sent to its sphere of action as soon as the employment of the Corps is decided upon. In the interest of the troops, only specialists should be attached to it.

The officer in charge of the supply stores must be able to move about, so that he can take personal action quickly should blocks occur. A small motor-car should, therefore, be allotted to him.

52. *Pioneer Parks and the Supply of Engineer Stores*

A special pioneer railhead for pioneer stores must be provided. In order to facilitate supervision and traffic, ammunition and food supplies should not be unloaded at this station if possible. Entire trains loaded with pioneer stores must be brought up to ensure an ample supply. This will also obviate the necessity of shunting at the stations in the zone of operations.

To enable him to send pioneer stores quickly up to the parks, the officer in charge of stores must have sufficient transport at his disposal; motor-lorries from the reserve depots are most suitable. Each Divisional Pioneer Park must have half a motor-lorry column at its disposal. Horse-drawn vehicles are only to be used in cases of emergency, owing to their limited capacity and speed.

In front of the Divisional Pioneer Parks, small regimental parks containing pioneer stores, rations, and the most important articles of equipment, must be pushed forward for the battle and established in convenient positions, distributed along the front immediately behind the trenches. The further forward these regimental parks are, the better for the fighting troops who have to fetch their material from them. They should be under the supervision of officers or senior non-commissioned officers. It is the duty of the regimental store officers to see that the parks are constantly kept filled.

IX. CLOTHING AND EQUIPMENT

53. *Steel Helmets*

The steel helmets, issued immediately before and during the battle, gained a great reputation among the troops in a very short time. It is considered desirable to equip artillery observers and anti-aircraft posts with steel helmets.

54. *Jackets and Footgear*

Owing to the fact that the buttons down the front of officers' jackets are now covered up, it is impossible to attach field glasses and pocket torches to them. For the assaulting parties lace boots and puttees proved satisfactory.

55. *Packs*

Generally speaking, the knapsack has proved superfluous in such critical fighting, both in defence and attack. The fighting kit is sufficient. A sandbag converted into a knapsack, in addition to the haversack and jacket and trouser pockets, has proved useful for taking a larger amount of supplies into the fighting line.

56. *Water Bottles*

It has been found necessary, during hard fighting, to supply infantry with large tin water bottles (capable of being slung) from the reserve depots, in order to carry a double supply of water, as infantry fighting in the front line suffers more from thirst than from hunger.

57. *Entrenching Tools*

Repeated requests from all arms for an increased supply of entrenching tools must be met by their provision from the reserve depots behind the battle sector.

58. *Hand Stereo-Telescopes*

It is very desirable that the troops be supplied with hand stereo-telescopes, as they are easy to carry, and are therefore more convenient than stereo-telescopes or semi-stereotelescopes for observers during heavy fighting.

59. *Maps*

The original supply of maps was insufficient, not only as regards quantity but also as regards detail. The latter was particularly apparent, owing to the fact that during the unfavourable conditions for observing which prevailed, firing had at first to be carried out chiefly by the map. Even if it could not be expected that all the numerous battery positions (which in comparison to the original front in June, are well behind the line) could be reconnoitred and fixed beforehand, it would nevertheless have been of advantage if a large number of points on the ground in question had been fixed and inserted on the maps. The subsequent supply of maps was also inadequate.

60. *Illuminating Material*

Arrangements can be made for the troops to have at their disposal a sufficient supply of illuminating material, by the issue of a certain quantity from the reserve supply of paraffin, lights, and spare batteries for electric pocket lamps. For the artillery, illumination is absolutely essential when firing at night, to enable it to distinguish the reference points, to set fuses, etc.

X. Horses and Vehicles

61. *Horses and Vehicles*

The horses have stood their strenuous exertions comparatively well. This may be attributed to the fact that oats were available in considerable quantities.

The supply of horses and vehicles to the troops has reached the utmost limits owing, on the one hand, to the permanent reduction in the establishment of horses and, on the other hand, to the permanent increase in fighting material and articles of equipment.

For bringing up trench material and sending forward food and ammunition at times when there are heavy demands for transport, it is very desirable that Divisions should be allotted motor-lorries and sections of horse-drawn columns from the reserve supply.

In the case of machine guns, the absence of spare horses, which had been struck off the establishment, was badly felt. In one machine gun company all the riding horses, including that of the Company Commander, had, owing to the lack of spare horses, to be used as draught horses.

XI. Food Supply

62. *Rations*

It is necessary that fresh troops going into the line, when the precise state of the battle is uncertain, should be supplied with the 3rd iron ration. All troops were unanimous in their request for increased supplies of bread, rusks, sausage, tinned sausages, tinned fat bacon, tinned and smoked meat, and tobacco, in addition. There was also urgent need for solidified alcohol for the preparation of hot meals.

In various quarters, the necessity for a plentiful supply of liquid refreshments of all kinds, such as coffee, tea, cocoa, mineral waters, etc., is emphasised still more. On the other hand, the supply of salt herrings, which increase the thirst, was found to be, as a general rule, very undesirable. There is no necessity for an issue of alcoholic drink in warm and dry weather.

Similar requests for improved rations, suited to the prevailing conditions, when in position, were made by the artillery.

63. *Canteen Stores*

The fact that individual batteries of a field artillery *Abteilung* are often, for tactical reasons, some little distance apart, and the supply wagons are engaged in bringing up rations, has the result that the field artillery is in a less favourable position than the infantry as regards the supply of canteen stores, which are carried on the supply wagons of the *Abteilung* staffs. A large number of other units, by regulation, carry no canteen stores with them, and have to depend upon the friendly assistance of other troops. It is therefore necessary, on principle, that infantry units should allow the sale of canteen goods to artillery units, etc.

64. *Ration Supply*

No special difficulties arose. The supply columns proved sufficient. The Corps arranged for rations to be brought up to the Divisional depots.

65. *Carrying up Rations*

The formation of carrying parties (*see* also para. IV. B. 32) was of great use in bringing up rations and also in supplying troops with ammunition and stores. Wherever infantry pioneer companies were not used for this purpose, those carrying parties were formed within companies; this has the advantage of the feeling of camaraderie which prevails between such carrying parties and their fighting troops.

During a battle, it is advisable to provide each battery with four "food-carriers" from the reserve supplies.

XII. Medical Services

66. *Reliefs*

The medical units of the Corps went into the line with the Divisions. The reliefs necessitated by this proved very useful, and this arrangement is preferable to taking over medical units already in the line and belonging to other Corps, when the latter are relieved. The duties of the medical services during continuous fighting in trench warfare are so strenuous, that the medical personnel urgently requires relief at the same time as the troops. Furthermore, the medical personnel takes greater pleasure in its difficult task and carries it out with more devotion if it is assisting the formation to which it belongs.

The relief of a field ambulance presents, it is true, many difficulties. It is best for the incoming personnel to arrive in the morning and for the outgoing personnel to leave during the afternoon of the same day. Should both parties be spending the night in the same place, the outgoing personnel must, if necessary, bivouac, in order that the quarters may be at the disposal of the personnel on duty.

67. *Motor-Ambulances*

The attaching of a motor-ambulance column to the Army Group proved itself very useful. In this connection it was found sufficient to place only a small proportion of the cars at the disposal of the casualty clearing stations (*Hauptverbandplätze*). The majority must be kept together so as to have a supply of cars available for use wherever they are most needed for the moment. This motor-ambulance reserve was principally used to transport cases to hospital trains.

68. *Stretcher Bearers*

It was of great advantage that before the Corps was sent into line, 50 stretcher bearers had been trained in each of the Divisional Field Recruit Depots, and were still there at the time the Corps went in. The great demand for stretcher bearers, which was universal, was in this way met to a certain extent.

69. *Communication between Medical Units*

Telephone communications also assumed great importance in consequence of the wide distribution of the medical arrangements. It is desirable that the Regulations should point out the importance of having ample telephone communications between all the various medical units in the line, so that these are not neglected until all the other telephone communications have been provided.

XIII. BILLETING AND TRAFFIC BEHIND THE FRONT

70. *Billeting*

Owing to troops in the front line being constantly relieved, a frequent change of Town-Majors was necessary. In the case of extensive billeting, difficulties occurred owing to Town-Majors having first to acquaint themselves with the billeting conditions whenever troops moved in, and, further, agricultural products, special buildings and orders in force could not be properly handed over. Permanent Town-Majors must be appointed for villages in the areas in which the columns and trains are working, and in the rear portions of the Divisional billeting areas.

At times when there is no great activity at the front, arrangements must be made for the construction of large wooden sheds in the back areas to accommodate men and horses.

71. *Military Police*

The police service behind the front is of the utmost importance. During any protracted fighting, men of sufficient authority and energy should be posted on all roads leading to the rear from the battle zone. Points of concentration for suspects should be arranged by the Divisions as close as possible to the dressing stations and casualty clearing stations. In the villages behind the fighting line, not only should there be a strict control on all exits, but an internal control should also be inaugurated. Detailed regulations should be issued by the Town-Major, who will appoint sergeant-majors and other personnel for carrying out this service.

72. *Road Traffic*

Regulation of traffic on all roads is the duty of the Field Mounted Police, assisted by cavalry. Each Division should have at least one through road allotted to it whenever possible.

XIV. RAILWAYS

73. *Railway Buildings*

The fighting front of the Army Group Stein (later Armin) was at first dependent on the railway station at Bapaume for the whole of its supplies. This station was complete and well constructed. During the first days of the operations, the railway buildings came under fire; trains could only run into Bapaume during the night, and the detraining station could no longer be used. The stations under construction further to the rear were not yet complete. In addition to the detraining stations required in normal times, well constructed detraining stations must be provided so far back that, even if the first or second line has to be abandoned, the enemy's artillery will not be able to shell them (about 13 kilometres).

Even in quiet times, all railway construction must be carried out from this point of view, taking into consideration the fact that, during operations on a large scale, at least three times the usual number of men must be provided for. The wish expressed by the troops that railways should be provided to facilitate the transport of material to the front line trenches, and that the pioneer depots, sawmills, etc., which in normal times are close to the front, should be connected by railways, is easily understood. On no account, however, should comprehensive railway establishments further in rear be neglected; during the battle period these ensure supplies, although during quiet periods their importance is not so apparent.

All such railway stations must be provided with long sidings for ammunition, pioneer, supply and hospital trains. In addition, each siding will be provided with good roads to and from it, and good dumping places.

74. *Detraining Personnel*

During important operations, the detraining personnel must be permanent. The changes in commanders and men detailed from the front for this duty, caused by the continual reliefs of the fighting troops, had a very disturbing effect, and every one of these men is urgently required in the front line. The work at the detraining stations requires a staff with knowledge of local conditions, under the leadership of an experienced and energetic official. Insufficient staff is the cause of slow detraining, congestion at the stations, and blocks in the traffic along the whole section of the line.

One officer provided with a motor-car must be made responsible for the whole of the detraining arrangements.

(Signed) SIXT v. ARMIN,
General Officer Commanding.

Books To Be Read Now

THE LAND OF DEEPENING SHADOW: GERMANY-AT-WA·
By D. Thomas Curti·
Revealing the Germany of *fact* in place of the Germany of *tradition;* telling t·
truth about Germany-in-the-third-year-of-the-war. 12mo. Net $1.·

I ACCUSE! (J'ACCUSE!)
By A Germa·
An arraignment of Germany by a German of the German War Party. Facts ev·
neutral should know. 12mo. Net $1·

THE RED CROSS IN FRANCE
By Granville Barke·
The popular playwright-author at his best; delightfully introduced by the F·
Joseph A. Choate. 12mo. Net $1·

SOULS IN KHAKI
By Arthur E. Coppin·
(With a foreword by General Bramwell Booth.) A personal investigation i·
the spiritual experiences and sources of heroism among the lads on the firing ·
12mo. Net $1·

BETWEEN ST. DENIS AND ST. GEORGE
By Ford Madox Hueffer
A discussion of Germany's responsibility and France's great mission—with t·
"respects" of the author to George Bernard Shaw. 12mo. Net $1.·

ONE YOUNG MAN
Edited by J. E. Hodder Williams
The experiences of a young clerk who enlisted in 1914, fought for nearly t·
years, was severely wounded, and is now on his way back to his desk.
12mo. Net $0·

WHEN BLOOD IS THEIR ARGUMENT
By Ford Madox Hueffer
This powerful, deep-probing exposition of German ideals is by an accep·
authority. 12mo. Net $1·

GERMAN BARBARISM
By Leon Maccas
A detailed picture of the German atrocities—indisputable and amazing—based ·
tirely on documentary evidence. By a neutral. 12mo. Net $1·

COLLECTED DIPLOMATIC DOCUMENTS
The original diplomatic papers of the various European nations at the outbre·
of the war. Quarto. Net $1·

THE ROAD TO LIEGE
By M. Gustave Somvil·
The work of the German "destruction squads" just over the German front·
(From German evidence.) 12mo. Net $1.·

MY HOME IN THE FIELD OF HONOUR
By Frances Wilson Huar·
·he simple, intimate, classic narrative which has taken rank as one of the f·
·guished books produced since the outbreak of the war.
Illustrated. 12mo. Net $1·

·. H. DORAN COMPANY   *Publishers*   New Yor·
·e In America for HODDER & STOUGHTO·